"Opening this book is like finding a vintage Garcia spade bit under the floorboards of the old barn. Kingdon delivers a rare gift; a glimpse into the real lives of 'big outfit cowboys'. These tough men and women devote their long days to the pursuit of great horses, cattle, dogs, country, gear and honing their skills while protecting the Cowboy Way work ethic. As the author's true tales unfold, the connecting thread is freedom...the unbridled freedom one can only find in this amazing, yet sometimes painful, hidden world. Respect, dignity and God are other recurring elements, especially evident in the wonderfully poignant Circle S cow story. But the real butter on the biscuit lies in Kindgon's insightful quotes sprinkled generously among the pages, borne of deep reflection on his own challenging journey and solidified during countless silent hours trotting a long circle back to camp. Kingdon and his peers achieve a special level of connectivity with themselves, the critters and the land, and this book does a splendid job of saddling a spare horse for the reader so they, too, can come along for at least part of the ride."

–Tim O'Byrne, Publisher/Editor, *Working Ranch* magazine

"Working as a big-outfit cowboy on the vast Northern Range, Miles Kingdon experienced things most people can't even imagine like gathering wily cattle on rough, remote ranches, spending time alone in the quiet of cow camp, encountering bears and predators face-to-face, riding through blizzards and deep snow, and walking away from a myriad of wrecks. He shares short vignettes from his cowboying days in this special little volume full hair-raising excitement, a bit of humility and insightfulness, and plenty of good old cowboy humor. As ranching evolves through time, Kingdon's authentic stories become timeless tales that document and preserve an era where deals were sealed with a handshake, reputations were earned with hard work and integrity, and a cowboy relied most on his instincts and his partnership with his horse and dog. Throughout the book readers not only come to respect Kingdon as a hard-core cowboy who gets the job done, but also as a skilled horseman who honors the horses from which he's learned."

–Jennifer Denison, Senior Editor, *Western Horseman*

"Escape in to a world that millions of people have dreamt about pursuing and savour the western ranch lifestyle with Miles Kingdon in his new book Beyond the Next Ridge. Many of us that have had the privilege of knowing Miles and rode alongside him have treasured the lessons and the laughs you will get because of his unique life. A window into a journey that few people ever really get to know. Cowboys lives have been portrayed in movies and glamorized in Hollywood to give us a sense of what it is like but in this book these stories with all their realities and rawness come from a person that has lived it and lived it fully. Spending a large portion of his time looking at the world from the back of a horse is a rare perspective in today's age. Sharing a personal story that is relatable for all of us who have had dreams, fears and successes Miles brings these experiences to life in this book for all of us to sense what it was like to be there. A must read!"

–Jonathan Field, Jonathan Field Horsemanship

"Miles Kingdon is a colourful character and the stories in his new book are just as colourful. Mike Rose said in the forward "… allowing you to share the story as if you were there too" and these words alone say a lot about what the reader will experience when reading this new book. Miles shares some very personal, private, emotional, and I think, hard to talk about stories and he also shares stories that were fun, and often hilarious. Stories of the dogs, horses, cattle, and cowboys he's worked with over the years at some of the biggest ranches in BC including the Gang Ranch and Douglas Lake Ranch. The near-death experiences have you on edge and some of the funnier stories have you in tears. I've said for years I wish more cowboys would write down and share their experiences and I was happy to see Miles do exactly that."

– Mark McMillan, President, BC Cowboy Heritage Society; Chair, BC Cowboy Hall of Fame

I love the beginning of each story where Miles gives us a glimpse into his big heart. Everyone who has been privileged to know him has to love him.

–Janet Normand

Beyond the Next Ridge

A Cowboy's Story

Miles Kingdon

Illustrations by Rob Dinwoodie

Beyond the Next Ridge – A Cowboy's Story

Copyright © 2018 by Miles Kingdon

ISBN: 978-1-9994794-0-4

Printed and bound in Canada by Blitzprint Inc.

Cover Design and Photos by Kim Taylor

Dedication

This book is dedicated to all the men and women who have, and still do, make their living with horses, or spend a big part of their life with them.

Table of Contents

Foreword

The storyteller's art is not in telling a good story, it is in the telling. It's not the humorousness of the story, or the subject of the story. No, a true storyteller imbues the tale with the feelings, the sounds, the smells, the joy, the grief...in short, the true storyteller shares the experience of the events, allowing you into their life, allowing you to share the story as if you were there too. This is the gift that Miles possesses. In these vignettes, he takes you with him to places in his life which reside forever in his memory, and lets you feel them as he has. The dreams of a child, of a young boy, of a teenager, of an independent young man, a cowboy. The stories tally up to what has been (so far), a life in touch, not just with his surroundings, but with life itself: the people, the animals, the weather... The storyteller takes no small risk in opening his life to the inspection of strangers. It takes great confidence to allow yourself to be examined, studied, and viewed dispassionately by people from all walks of life, never meeting them, yet they are "meeting" you. Do they like you? Do they believe you? These are questions which must tumble through the writer's thoughts as he presents himself to the reading world.

Having "grown up" with Miles (punctuation intended) and shared in no small number of a few stories which will, of necessity, remain unpublished, I would like to invite you, reader, to share a few of Miles' stories with him. When you read, involve yourself. Smell the pine-pollen , its tangy scent and lemony powder, listen to the dogs toenails clicking on the scarred linoleum, feel the stabbing cold of the wind powering through the narrow valley...enjoy. I did.

Gratefully, Mike Rose

Acknowledgements

I consider myself fortunate for all the men and women I have ridden with over many ranges. All of you know who you are; there are so many. As well, those others visited and spent many good times with. I have learned something from everyone I've ever spent time with.

I look back at my years on the outfits and feel I have been truly blessed to have spent time with Jesse, Adam and Riley; our little cowboys. As well, our daughters Shannon and Emily. I'm proud to have been able to ride beside them all and pass on what knowledge I could in a short time...you have enriched my life.

I often think of, and am thankful for, the chance to know all those cows in the herd that came and went over the years, making room for their offspring to take their place. And all the horses who carried me to my many adventures, and back home again. And the dogs that wanted only to be in the thick of it with me...Thank you.

A special thanks to my wife, Possum, who rode many miles beside me and helped me on a lot of tough jobs. She was the cactus in my boot, telling me to write. My parents, brother, daughters, friends, in-laws, all told me to write, but Possum was relentless. This is our book.

To Rob Dinwoodie, who phoned me that snowy day at Christmas, whose interest in this project really was the final straw to add momentum; thanks for your wonderful illustrations and support. Ken Mather, you have my respect. Your own compositions have been a guideline for me. Thanks for your advice and editing and the huge part played in making this happen. Kim Taylor, incredible photographer and much more; many, many thanks for your unerring eye. Murphy and Katharine Shewchuk, thanks for your advice and support. Tim, Chris and Mark O'Byrne. You have always really been there for us. Much more than just friends to lean on. Bev and Larry Ramstad, you took Tonya, Shannon and I in, and helped us start over again.

To all the people in the Dog Creek and Canoe Creek districts, and from all over, for your caring and support. We will be forever thankful. You have all been a part of the process, the trail that led to this book. I can truly say I have been blessed with a great life.

Introduction

REFLECTIONS OF A COWBOY'S LIFE AHORSEBACK

"I like to think that most folks will connect with one or more of these wanderings or meanderings of a cowboy's mind, as he travelled along the trail for camp with his spurs and jingle bobs chiming in time to his horse's stride... a pulse of my lifetime spent going places on a horse..."

"Now I understand a bit more of why the cow stands in the creek, or beside it, with some of her sisters, long after she has drunk her fill...that rhythm...water babbling and gurgling merrily on its way. A rhythm not unlike the rhythm felt when she was in her mother. That rhythm was as necessary to her as her fill of the water was...we have to wonder...what do we get from the rhythm...where does it take us?"

Chapter One
Understanding the Horse Better

" 'Fixing a horse.' But is it, really? Each time I come into a relationship between man and beast, I think less and less about myself, or anyone else 'fixing' a critter. It is something akin to that, but when applied to relationships, it should have a lighter tone, a different shade; maybe adjusting the approach. Each of these situations require a quiet time, a time for remembering, or at the very least, a time of listening. And searching for that feel."

I think back to my boyhood days, growing up (at least I think I grew up), on our family farm in south Saskatchewan. My brother and I were free to roam the farm and explore. As we got older, we ventured out across those grasslands of prairie wool and government pastures between our farm and the U.S. border. When we weren't riding horses out there, we were dreaming of horses, leaving my brother and I with many fond memories of those years.

Like most kids of that era, of course I can only speak for myself, I imagined myself six-foot tall, a lanky cowboy with hard eyes and a cat-like stance. Like the ones the western novels portrayed, those "Lords of the Plains". I saw myself out punchin' cows or riding the windswept plains on my black gelding. Sometimes it would be a buckskin, sometimes a bay; colors varied from day to day...I just wanted to be a cowboy.

Well, I fell short of the six foot mark a bit, and as for the 'hard eyes' and 'cat-like stance', I don't know what happened there, either. But I know the important thing is, I became a cowboy. I spent the rest of my life going places ahorseback.

That beautiful little farm where we grew up was a place to not only learn to work, and look after our crops and livestock, but also a place to daydream of the life I would eventually live. I remember hearing the cowboys trailing cattle in the government pasture across the fence from our farm. I would stand in our yard the entire time, motionless, and watch them trailing along, hearing the occasional yell.

I've not seen a mirage since those days, but I saw them back then, and they've been etched in my mind ever since. My imagination would run wild, as it should with a child. I would see myself as one of those trail hardened hands, enduring the heat and dust with my trusty horse.

The herds of cattle I saw, strung out, shimmering in the sunlight, with the cowboys chousing them along would be a slow moving line on the horizon, some two miles away. Suddenly, this sight would loom up as though they were a half mile away from me. Then, that vision would  gradually shrink back to a small, slow moving line on the horizon once again. Which was where that little boy, standing in the middle of the prairie farm, wanted to be.

Thanks to my brother and I, every horse on our farm, that would stand to be ridden, did see some country! Even old Peggy, our faithful workhorse. She was the last of the old teams on the farm, and when Mom and Dad went to tractors, she was the horse they kept, along with others we could ride. We rode Peggy everywhere. And she patiently put up with all we threw at her.

Dad didn't care to see the old girl sweated up from George and I playing cowboys and Indians on her. So my folks bought a pony for us that would take the brunt of our hard rides, and Peggy got a well-deserved break from our shenanigans. Mom named that pony Trixie, and she was full of tricks, like a lot of ponies are. We learned to duck as she ran us under the lower limbs of the maple tree behind the barn when she'd had enough of our 'hard cowboyin'. It seemed like we had a lot to learn to just get along with that little pony, but once we did, we were a lot wiser.

I can't recall how many times, when out riding alone, she would spin and run back to the barn; at times cutting a trail right through our precious strawberry patch. Mom saw this episode unfold one day, and once we had matters in hand, she walked over to check out her strawberries to see how much damage was done. She was quite surprised that those little hooves had not touched a plant.

I know I learned a lot about riding and finding a better way from working with that little pony. I put a lot of miles on her, and felt I was ready for any bronc that was handed to me. In my mind, Genghis Khan himself would have been amazed at my prowess ahorseback! And I'm sure George felt the same way.

From Trixie, we graduated to starting our own colts, under the guidance of Mom and Dad. Some of these colts that we raised on the farm were out of old Peggy. We got quite the education. It's hard to imagine what direction our young lives would have taken if we hadn't been raised around horses. From spring to late fall, we rode all over the prairie. And even though we could see all around us because of the flat terrain, we went 'there' anyway.

When we went visiting neighbours, or when we had company, we were sure to hush up and bend our ears when the conversation turned to horses. I guess that was the wonderful thing about not having good television reception all the time; people visited, and they told stories.

Even though I was hungry for cowboy stories, and I did get some of them occasionally, those horse stories told were most often about teams of horses. My family was made up of teamsters. They rode horses as well, but it was the teams that did all the work at one time, and not that long ago.

Same as the neighbours; most everyone used teams.

And runaways with teams and wagons, I was to learn, could be more frightening than a runaway ahorseback. And, why some horses that could pull heavier loads for, seemingly, one teamster more than they could for another, left me in awe of a person's ability with horses.

Another subject that was often the conversation of people in that era and place; a subject that was to mean more to me as time went on, was that of the horse coming through for people in a blizzard. Blizzards like they used to have before the 70's, I guess.

It seemed like everyone had a story or two about a team of horses finding their way home; in the dark as well, long after the driver had come to the realization that they might not make it home. My parents had many stories like that.

When them old Saskatchewan storms drifted roads closed, there was just no way of telling where the road was, or where the ditch was. Sometimes, there'd be fence posts visible that you could follow, if the snow wasn't blowing too bad. But many times visibility was all but gone. At night, the only thing to guide you would be yard lights from the nearest farm. Again, that's if the snow wasn't blowing or drifting too bad.

My Dad used to walk the four miles to the coal mine where he worked, even in those times when a blizzard would drift the roads closed. It might be days until the road grader plowed the roads out. We would sure be glad to see that machine coming in the distance.

Dad said many a time he would look back and see the lamp burning in the kitchen window, and would want to come back to the warm house, heated by the coal stove. But he'd put one foot in front of the other and find his way through the dark to the mine to make another dollar.

I often wondered what our mom went through, watching him get swallowed up by the darkness. Praying he'd not get lost out on the prairie in the blizzard; an occurrence that happened frequently during those prairie winters.

And that's where old Peggy came in. Dad eventually got some hay to the mine shop. I guess when the road was opened up again, he would have hauled some hay there with the '46 International one ton, our only vehicle at the time. That way, when the next storm rolled in, as inevitably it would, he would ride Peggy

13

to work bareback, and let her eat hay in the shop till it was time for him to come home. No fear of getting lost with a horse. Their homing instinct is unerring. Nighttime, blizzard, or what have you; horses will bring a person home.

It seemed almost every farming family on the prairies, and likely everywhere, had similar stories to ours. Many people entrusted their lives to their horses' unfailing sense of direction, enabling them to get home safe and sound.

My parents told me a story of a neighbour who received a phone call from a farmer on up the road, asking him if he had noticed their friend's car go past. They had been on their way home during a blizzard. He said he had not. As the day was giving itself over to evening, the farmer wasted no time in hitching up a team, and off he went, in search of his friends.

Sure enough, he found them sitting in their car a couple miles away, stuck in a snow drift. The storm was really picking up steam, and it was getting dark as he loaded the couple up in his sleigh, and headed for home.

He knew it was wise to let the horses find their way, as it was impossible to see anything. They'd travelled a while and it wasn't until he saw their own fresh sleigh tracks that he came to realize they'd been going in a circle. He made a decision then that was to possibly save their lives.

The team was taking them past a straw stack, so he stopped on the downwind side and told the couple to get off and hollow out a nest in the side of the stack. They then snuggled in there to wait for morning.

Come first light, they crawled out and looked around, as the storm was now over. The farmer could see his own house not a half mile away. They had, he realized, spent the night in his own straw stack. Upon examining the horse tracks, the farmer realized why they'd been circling. The problem was that one horse was walking faster than the other. This wouldn't have happened had the team been more evenly matched. That man never did drive that team together again, but hitched them with other horses that were more evenly matched.

Anyone who has ever ridden horses to work, or going places, will sooner or later have similar situations arise. They will find themselves needing the horse to find their way, which they will, if they trust in the horse.

My Dad told me a story about his Uncle John Graham, who was one of the best teamsters Dad ever saw at work. He really liked his horses and they liked him back. Apparently, the broncs that nobody else wanted, or couldn't hitch up, would eventually end up with Uncle John, who would soon be getting along fine with them.

My Dad had that same knack as well, and Mom talks about her Dad, my Diedo, working with snuffy horses like that. Anyways, Uncle John had muscular dystrophy. Dad reckons it took about five or six years for it to get real bad. It got to where even scratching his head was difficult.

The doctor told Uncle John to stay away from the horses, knowing full well horses would mean work for Uncle John, which would only aggravate his condition. But he loved his horses, and that, simply, was his life. He had Clydesdale/Percheron cross teams, mostly horses he had raised himself. Uncle John was about 55 years old and not in very good shape. But that didn't slow him down much, and one day he was out plowing the field with a team of three abreast. He had a bay mare that had been a bit too snorty for the other teamsters, hooked on the left side while he was plowing. Later on, when he'd finished for the day, he'd unhooked the plow, and was walking behind his team back to the barn.

Meanwhile, my Dad, Great Grandma, Uncle Tom, and other relatives happened to be at the farm that day, finishing up chores. They noticed that the team had stopped about a hundred yards from the barn, and were wondering what Uncle John was doing. Then the team started walking again, but that bay mare would only take little steps, forcing the other two to keep a slower pace, and she had her head bent back to the left a bit.

In the short time it took the team to walk slowly up to the barn, the family realized Uncle John was dragging on the ground with the left rein attached to his hand, beside the bay mare. They went over to help, and got the story.

As he told it; he'd fallen down as he was walking behind the team, and was unable to get to his feet again. Not having anything else he could have done, he wrapped that left line around his wrist and spoke to his bay, telling her to 'geddup', and she did. But she knew something was wrong and would only take little short and slow steps.

Ordinarily, when horses hear something dragging along beside them, the urge is very strong to start trotting to leave that sound behind. A trot becomes a gallop real quick! But that mare knew something was wrong and was very careful with Uncle John behind her. Understandably, because when you think about it, Uncle John was kind and confident with his horses and they had trust in him.

"Loneliness has been the doorway to a room where Reverie resides. I have been, and am, thankful for moments of reverie, which have helped me to balance thoughts and emotions, and find an inner peace. And Faith and Freedom have been the light outside the door so I may find my way back out of that room again. Faith shows me what awaits us beyond this dimension: another dimension, a split second away and well worth the wait. But first, I must complete my schooling."

Throughout my years going places on the horse, and working stock horseback, there have been many times when I needed to trust the horse's instinct and know-how to get me through a situation. Sometimes I listened to the horse, sometimes I didn't. In my younger days, if I figured I knew best, I'd go with my plan like most young cowboys. At times, it could be costly to me and my mount. A couple of those deals later, and I was eager for my horse's second opinion on the subject.

One time at the Gang Ranch, my horse and I rode through one of those tough spots on the trail. It was late in the fall, and we had quite a cold snap of weather roll in on us. It was the end of October and usually that time of year is not full blown winter, but being close to the mountains like we were, a winter front can blow in and make you feel just like it was the middle of January.

This winter front rolled in on us real slow. One day it was minus 15 C, and the next day a little colder and so on, until about five days later I woke up and it was minus 35 C. Down in the hollow like P & T Camp was, there was no wind, but it was cold just the same.

We were headed out that day to gather Home Ranch Valley to bunch the herd of about 450 up and sort off the bulls and thin cows. Cory, Ryan, and Rafael would trail them to headquarters. The remaining cows, about 400 head, would get trailed up to Fosberry Meadows the next day, where Merv was keeping another thousand head rustled out on the meadows.

Cory Newton, Ryan Fritz and Rafael Horsch had been down to headquarters a few days before, and from their apartments had traded their fall clothes for winter clothes, fortunately for them. I had not had the same opportunity yet, but I had a second neckrag to put under my hat to cover my ears, and a good lined denim jacket and lined boots, so I figured nothing else to do but ride out and get it done.

We rode out just as dawn was breaking. As we crested the brow of the hill and hit the flats, we felt that wind hit us. There was a storm brewing which reminded me of a good old Saskatchewan blizzard in the making. If I hadn't been so cold, I'd of felt right at home. The wind was at our backs as we rode to the east, and we fanned out on our own circles to bunch the stock up. As cold as it was, we straggled very few in to the rodear grounds. Most everything was already bunched up in two or three tight herds in the timber; waiting out the storm, for a storm it had become. She was blowing in from the mountains like it meant business.

It was tough to break into the herd. The critters milled around, trying to get back to the timber; as we had them bunched up at the edge of an aspen grove, doing our best to get a good sort on them.

About an hour of parting off bulls and thin cows had pretty much gotten everything out that needed extra grub. The boys headed out with that small herd of about 60 head. With the wind at their backs, I felt a bit better about having them on the move. As they rode away, I hollered above the howl of the wind not to be bashful about lighting a fire once the trail took them into the timber country—not that they needed telling! Those bulls and cows knew full well where headquarters and the haystacks were, and wouldn't need any persuasion to get there, so a little fire to warm up the boys would be much appreciated.

Bev and Larry Ramstad, the managers, were going to rendezvous with the boys where the timber met the open grasslands, above Gaspard Creek, with the pickup, and bring hot soup. I figured they should all be down at headquarters in about four to five hours, putting them there at about 2pm or so.

The rest of our herd made a dash back into the timber to wait out the storm. And me, I turned my horse's nose to the west and headed into the wind, back to camp. I had about two and a half or three miles to go, which wasn't far at all really, but as cold as I was, it sure seemed longer. I didn't want to waste any more time in the open country, and was looking forward to hitting the timber and getting some relief from the wind in my face.

The horse I was riding was about 15.1 hands, and not very heavily muscled. She was a nice looking brown mare, really built for travelling, and that's what she liked to do. Ken Hoffman had started her as a four year old, and had done a good job on her. As I recall she was a bit odd, in that, when he ran her into the corrals, she'd been the kind of horse to hang out by herself. A lot.

Then Nolan Ferris rode her to work as a five year-old, earlier that year in May, when we started trailing herds to summer range. I remember Nolan putting some tough rides on her for the first couple of weeks. But when she lined out, she really was a mile-eating mount.

She'd been turned out for a couple of months with the open string to have a rest. I was needing to change up some of my horses, so I pulled her out and shod her up. It'd be good to keep her coming ahead rather than be a handful for a cowboy next spring. One who maybe wasn't as handy as Nolan.

Her name was Hong Kong. Nolan had done a good job on her, but if a cowboy wasn't careful, she'd be quick to break into a walk, and real fast break into a trot just as soon as that left boot hit the stirrup. It was something Nolan had spent a lot of time on; getting her better…but she was a different kind of horse, and no telling when she would take off because she was always on coiled springs and ready to go.

Riding Hong Kong back facing that wind was a bit rough, and no sooner had we made it into the timber and onto the trail for

18

camp, that I started to feel warm. And that's when I knew I was really starting to freeze up. I stopped Hong Kong and stepped off her to start walking, which would help me warm up. There was about 16-18 inches of snow on the ground and I thought to myself that would give me a good workout.

But after plodding on for no more than 30 or 40 feet, I realized it was all I could do to put one foot in front of the other. I was already suffering the effects of hypothermia. I recall my mind had started to panic; something which had not happened to me in quite a while. I stopped and thought for a moment about my situation, and realized what a mistake I'd made by getting off my horse. Now the only thing that was likely to save me was to get back in the saddle, give Hong Kong her head, and hang on.

The problem was, I needed to get back in the saddle. As good a horse as she was to ride, she had still been a bit of a fiddle foot, and a bit busy when I went to climb aboard earlier. With hypothermia, a person has very little muscle control over their entire body, and I really didn't think I could make it up there. But I had to try.

I gathered up the reins, got my foot in the stirrup, and got both hands back on the saddle horn. I pulled with all my strength, but neither my hands or arms could do much at all. My hands slipped off the horn before I was even halfway up there. My mind was becoming frantic, trying to get my body to do more, but the muscles could not respond. It is a very strange thing to have happen.

My mind couldn't accept that my body just would not react and as my left foot slipped out of the stirrup again, I stood there looking at my saddle, wanting to be back in it again. A place that had been my home for so long and I couldn't get up there. How many times, I thought to myself, had I been okay, as long as I was in the old 'hurricane deck', no matter what the storm?

So many thoughts went through my mind in such a short time. I marvelled at how well the mind functioned, and yet my body had become a useless thing.

Then a peace came over me. I was feeling no pain at all. It was a pretty little meadow where Hong Kong and I had stopped. I remembered seeing this spot in the summer, and it brought to mind the peace I had felt then.

There is no good way to continue this story, as it would be a waste of paper, ink and thought process to not tell of the thoughts and emotions that overwhelmed me at that moment. This story would appear as a half-truth without the rest.

My thoughts turned to my sons, our boys. Jesse, Adam, and Riley had crossed the veil to the next dimension, a short two years before. They were already there waiting for me. I remember saying a prayer to God. I wanted to go where my boys were. It was such a peaceful little spot to be in; and I was ready to cross over. This was not a giving up, rather a fleeting glimpse, a step towards the strange, yet calm place of total acceptance. I was not scared.

I don't know where my thoughts would have taken me from there, because I felt a bump on my right arm. I had been standing with my right side to this mare, as I had looked around at this aspen grove, this peaceful place. Hong Kong had then nudged me with her muzzle. I looked at her and she had her head bent back towards me, just watching me. Then she did it again. The first time, I couldn't be sure she'd bumped me, in that place of reverie where I was. But the second time seemed to really make me aware.

And then the thought occurred to me; she had not moved a muscle when I had tried to climb aboard. She had been waiting for me. My mind came alive! I looked around me for ideas, a way to get in the saddle again. There in the snow before us, about twelve feet away, was a depression in the snow. A hole in the ground, likely a spot where the bulls root into the ground to douse themselves with dirt as protection against flies. Now filled with snow, it appeared as a slight depression.

I was able to lead Hong Kong forward the few steps it took for her to put her front feet in that hollow. She did what I asked of her without hesitation. This time, the saddle horn was not above my eye level, but about chest level. What a huge difference that made.

I tried to get on then and she waited patiently. I recall her muzzle give my left side a bump once again as I began my last try to get up. I was able to hook my chin on the saddle horn this time, and I crawled, clawed with powerless fingers that I finally locked together over the horn. When my right leg needed to swing over the saddle horn, I leaned my chest on the horn and reached back with my right hand to help my leg over the cantle. Then I was in.

I straightened up a bit, fearful of losing my balance, and my mare flicked an ear back at me. I spoke to her, saying "I'm here now. And I'm staying here." I guess I gave her a nudge and she walked through the bull wallow and out the other side, with careful steps, like she was walking on egg shells. We headed for camp.

She walked along for about a hundred yards or so, and then picked it up to a slow jig and kept that up all the way through the horse pasture. I remember being thankful that the slipwire was hung back and not shut. We made our descent into the yard and the catch pen. It was nice and still down in there, amidst the trees and bunkhouse. Hong Kong walked up to the little hay stack by the catch pen and grabbed a mouthful; she was glad to be here, as was I.

I managed to slip the headstall off her and made my way to the cook car. I had a real difficult time climbing the steps into the cook car, and luckily the cook opened the door for me. The simplest little jobs for my hands were near impossible. But it was warm in there, and the coffee was on.

It took a little time to get feeling better. But gradually, after a few cups of coffee, I was able to move my body like normal again, although it left me feeling sick to my belly for most of the day. I managed to swallow some soup after a while, and kept it down.

My thoughts at that point went to Dan Spaans up at Big Meadow Camp. Dan was rustling out about 650 head of weaned cows up there, and he had five cow/calf pairs straggled in from the mountain country. Using the ranch radio, I made plans with him to wean those calves off, and I would haul them down to headquarters.

I was not in any condition to ride any more that day, but doing something kept my mind off the ache in my belly and the one in my head. So I got in the pickup with the horse box on it, and headed over to Big Meadow Camp. By the time I got there, Dan already had the cows in and we parted off the calves and got them loaded.

I played out easily, but it sure helped to have something to do. Thinking back, during those moments when I had really thought I couldn't make it. For me was not a feeling I was accustomed to. My horse had come through for me. And something else more powerful came through for me; something many of us hesitate to talk about, but we all know of; God. He came through. Again. So there was this horse that He had put together with me...

The more I work with the horse, the more I think that the horse has a greater stake in our dealings with them than what we really pay attention to. I mean, for a cowboy, wherever he or she is, we get up early and work long days towards a goal. There is a schedule to adhere to. So, we saddle our horse, head out to work with them and we try to feel what's going on with the horse.

To feel where the horse is at. If we can go with that, our day may be more productive. But we get too busy at times, as always happens when working stock, and we miss little signs the horse gives out. And if we miss too many of them, business will really pick up. At times like that, the rider had best be 'forked' or they will be 'well grounded' soon.

As I get older and work with more horses, I find myself feeling for those little signs more often. To really search for that feel, like I did when I was a boy, riding across those sunny prairies, before I got so busy.

Some people may doubt the horse has thought processes. Some people may doubt that a horse is capable of actually thinking

22

about the human. But a great many people will not doubt those stories of how a horse had come to care for someone, for whatever reason. Horses can like you. They may like the work that they do with you. I know this is true of cowhorses.

My grandfather on my Mom's side, talked of what he did with his horses during the winter. He would keep a few horses at the farm for doing chores, hauling coal and going to town. All the rest he would turn loose on the prairie, after fall harvest, and they would stay out all winter. When winter got too rough, the valley was only about three miles south. There, the horses found plenty of shelter along the river and more than enough good prairie wool grass to keep them fleshed up.

Come spring time, all the loose horses would come back home again by themselves. They liked getting handled and liked getting fed their oats before and after work, but that wasn't important enough to them to come home throughout the long winter. They enjoyed their time away to see something different. But I think, as do many of the old timers, there was another reason why they came back by themselves. Why?

They were handled at home. They were brushed off and felt cared for as they ate their oats. And, when getting harnessed, they'd stand patiently with a contented look about them. Waiting for the word to step up, and step across that pole to get the yoke and traces hooked up. They had a purpose. They knew that, and they liked it.

They could stand out on those windswept hills above the river, with tails blowing against their hip and be quite content. But come springtime, something started gnawing at their mind; something they needed to do. And finally, after a few days of thinking about it, usually an older mare would point her nose for home and one by one, the rest would follow.

Chapter Two
The School of the Horse

"People often tell me that their horse gets really bothered when riding away from other horses. We realize they are a family animal, like many of us. But we must also remember that a horse will be a bit more comfortable leaving those other horses if they like the person they are with, and if that person emits an aura of confidence."

This is just some 'ruminations' of mine of my life ahorseback. We'll see what you think.

Funny how my hip feels so much better while I'm on a horse; even though it's twisted, and it hurts to walk sometimes, it feels natural when I'm on a horse. Now I know why the old cowboys could sit on a cowhorse so long, even though their bodies were beat up. Like our old friend, Hyde. Because they have spent so many years of their life in the saddle, it just gets formed to fit there.

Many different disciplines of riding revolve around the horse, and it's okay and maybe even healthy to be a student of more than one. But one posture and balance of the rider is right for riding the working cow horse, especially outside of the arena in rough country. The horse will tell you it's right.

Bruce Sandifer comes closer today than most, I think, when it comes to posture and balance of the rider in the style of the Californios (vaqueros). I have felt this same difference of riding posture makes a difference with the horse, and in how the horse responds, by years of riding the horse to cows over rough country.

I went to Santa Barbara, California, where this style of horsemanship was an era unto itself. I saw the environment and geography first-hand, though briefly, where tens of thousands of cattle were gathered, sorted and roped to trade hides and fatback in the real heyday of the Californios.

Those vaqueros and their mounts would have put in a hard days ride, and not have lost sight of the first hill they rode over that morning. Lots of up and down. Very similar to a lot of the cow country I've spent my life riding through.

I'm glad I had the opportunity to ride in that 'Californio' country. After all, that's what I've done all my life and will do much more of; ride and go places ahorseback and work cows in rough country.

I see now how riding horses in different environments needs a different method of riding and impacts muscle development in different ways. Possum and I have spent so many years riding a horse to cows that we couldn't really see the need to saddle up unless there were cows to gather or work; at least for a part of our lives. I can say for sure though, that I don't want to work cows unless I'm ahorseback. And after looking at the horses out in the meadows for a while, it didn't take long to saddle up and find something to do, somewhere to go.

It sure made me feel better inside and out. I love to live in a land where, in the early morning light, and the still of the fading light of day, I can hear a cow bawl up her calf.

Being on a horse is good for me, as I think it probably is for many people who have spent years horseback. Its good for the inner man even more…for the soul. That's why I've felt after all those years in the saddle, that the outside of the horse is good for the inside of me. And if I've thought of it that way, there's got to be someone else who has as well.

I have often, over the years, when in poor health or with broken limb, had the boys bring in a couple of those horses from my string which were my 'medicine horses'. Those that were really good for the inside of me, and smooth on my old shock absorbers. And no matter how poorly I felt beforehand, or whatever weight was on my shoulders, I always felt better for being on the back of a horse and going somewhere.

I've always tried to do the best I could at my work, as anybody does. Always tried to have something a bit better at the end of every day, or ride. But there would come those moments, all too often, when business really picks up (as it does from time to time when working livestock). And I'd get all wrapped up with the job at hand; whether it be running ornery or wild cattle out of rough country, or roping yearlings to doctor in the feed grounds with frozen hands. And I would not always pay close attention to keeping my hands light with the horse and keeping everything right with the horse.

Afterwards, I would beat myself up for having pulled on my horse's mouth or pushed him too much during those fast moments. But many rides later, as in 'NOW', I look back on it and see more of it as just how it was to be at that time. I'll explain why I see it this way.

Life is school. Once we are done grade school, we go on to high school, then maybe university for a few years. That doesn't mean we're done with school. Now I think it may be said that the last days of your post-secondary education is the first day of the rest of your schooling. Each mistake we make, and it may be better to not think of it as a mistake, but rather a situation that didn't turn out the way we hoped it would, might be viewed as just another class we had to take.

Once a person gets to that spot where we take that perspective, then there's a better chance that we will learn something from those instances. Some way of setting up a situation so that things work out better for us next time. We only need to get to that spot in our life where we realize that was just one more class that we needed to go through.

People beat themselves up way too much sometimes. We know we are trying to do the best that we can, the right thing. And what is the right thing? Having a situation turn out the way we wish it to, but it is inevitable that at times life will take its course and intervene maybe against our wishes, and it doesn't work out according to our plans. It was just meant to be. It is one more situation that we were meant to learn from; an opportunity for us to learn to deal with one more thing, to put a finer temper to that steel within us. And at times like that, we need to learn to forgive ourselves…God does. It's time to move on, get after something else.

I cherish the memories of growing up on my family's farm in Saskatchewan. I was always eager for any chance to do something with horses. My parents always had horses on the farm. Chore horses for feeding cows and cleaning barns in the winter months; and in summer trailing cows to grazing leases and back home again.

At night I would lie awake listening to the wind blowing or rubbing the branches of the old poplar trees against the house, and smell the comforting aroma of coal burning in the furnace, snug in my bed. I would dream of the days I would be working with a hard crew of old cowboys, spending long days in the saddle, and learning all there was to know about the reined stock horse.

And one day, my dreams were to come true. I would make my living that way. It became my life, my pastime, my dreams…and I wondered how this craft came to be; where was its beginnings? And I found out more of the vaqueros, the Californios who made up the biggest part of the crews that trailed the great herds of cattle up the west coastline to the grasslands of Oregon and Washington and into British Columbia.

The old photographs in books I saw, of the early herds trailed up the Okanagan Valley from Washington to British Columbia were of the vaqueros wearing and using the same gear and sitting a horse the same as in the photos of some of the old Californios...many similarities. I spent years chasing down that knowledge, and developing my own skill sets riding the stock horse to work on the big outfits.

Occasionally, I would travel back home to my folks's farm, and watch my Father doing things with the horse that I was only just discovering now; even though he was a teamster, and I made my living astride the horse. During those visits I would listen to stories my folks told of horses, and of jobs with horses that opened my mind and eyes to the fact that I could have learned much more in that environment without ever leaving the prairies that I loved so much. But that is life. This is where I was meant to live and make my living. And I had the proper start where my brother and I grew up.

Wherever there is a horse, there is an opportunity to get better with that horse. To understand that horse better. And no better way to understand that horse than to watch it. Be still and watch it. Then work with it. Feed cows with it, follow cows with it, ride it...lots…And though one might come off…and we all do…that's ok too. That's just part of it. It makes us wiser and helps us understand the horse better.

At times, I've been hurt while learning and getting acquainted with the horse. Still, I felt the desire grow stronger inside of me until out of my boyhood daydreams rode a crew of horsemen, riding out of the past, down a long trail before me. One rider stopped his horse and turned his head to look at me…through me, as if wondering if I would follow in his tracks.

And I now think that it's important for people to see us happy at what we do, and do it as well as we can, so that the young people watch us. And then, one day, I may be the rider that stops his horse and looks back through the dust into a younger person's eyes, knowing they want to follow in our tracks.

Chapter Three
Stubby and the Dog Tucker

"Now, after looking back over the years, I think there may be less right or wrong and more 'just how it is'."

When I cowboyed at Douglas Lake, one of the high points of the year was moving down to the Morton camp in the spring. After spending all winter with snow boots on, and moving herds of cattle from one camp to the next, where the feed was, or riding the feedlot with all the muck and slop that goes with roping in that environment, it was an understatement to say it was a welcome change to move down to the Morton.

The Morton was a cow camp on about 5,000 acres of grass. We trailed 1,500 Hereford cows down along the Nicola River to calve out there, usually about mid-March. The snow would mostly be gone by then, with water running everywhere from spring runoff, and the birds singing along the river bottom. It was great to get back into riding boots and spurs again, and shoe up a new string of horses for spring works.

The Morton camp consisted of several structures; one being an old log cabin with a sod roof. It was built by C.M. Beak, about 1880, awhile before Douglas Lake Cattle Company was formed. The crew stayed in this old cabin. It was built up on a bench, above an old barn and catch pen, or round corral; these being down on the river flat. Every spring we'd pull a cook car down for the cook to stay in and feed us up.

Once the cow herd was getting to where they were mostly calved out, we'd trail them across Douglas Lake Road and pair them off into the Howse Field, which was a piece of bunchgrass about the same size as the Morton. Then we'd deal with the 'ticks'; the Rocky Mountain wood tick. Tick season dictated that we ride full time across those hills checking stock; riding out on some four or five year-old colts that needed the miles, and looking for cows that were down with ticks. Then we'd pick ticks.

Some fellas would pack a little bean can or soup tin along, and pick ticks and burn them up in that can. When the bosses found this out, we changed those practices pretty quick, as nobody wants a grass fire. So there was not much else to do with the ticks but pick and squish…

If you get the right female, usually along the poll or upper neck region, that cow will generally make it to her feet and wander off. She'd be a bit tipsy, but alive nonetheless. For it is the female tick that emits a toxin into the bloodstream, causing temporary paralysis, and unless that tick, maybe more, is picked off, the cow will not regain her feet.

You will get the odd cow, once in a while, that'll just not get up again; whether you didn't find the 'right' tick, or she'd just been down and paralyzed way too long. Those you usually end up putting down; if they're not dead already. And some springs, the ticks are more active than others. Between that, and some calving problems, there's always a few cows that won't make it to branding season. And if the cowboys have a dog back at camp, they'll usually haul a leg or two off one of those sometimes 'aged' beef, back home for their dog buddy. Dog tucker.

One year, myself, our foreman, John Young, Rock Creek, and Ed Roberson, were camped at the Morton. Not to forget about Pam Berard, in the cook car, who kept our bellies full…I was quite excited being the kid on the crew, to be part of this crew of top hands.

John was a good foreman; always forgiving of our mistakes, easy to work for, and kind to man and beast. Ed was, I guess, not quite feral, but a little rough around the edges. The guy would ride anything with hair, and was quick with a rope. Rock Creek, whose real name was Tom Dynneson, came from a place called Rock Creek, so that was his moniker. He was another hand you wanted in your corner when business picked up. Sure knowledgeable, and a memory like a steel vault. If he saw it once, it was locked away; if he heard the cow count, it was locked away. All good guys to ride with.

Ed had a good pack of trail hounds, and when he rode at the Morton, he'd keep them staked out along the river about half a mile from camp. That way they couldn't keep the camp awake at night with their baying at something they heard or winded, or maybe at the coyotes hanging too close.

Most hounds, if they're any good, use their nose a lot and their mouth just about as much. It's what they're supposed to do. The hound's mouth tells the handler a lot about where they are when trailing bears or what have you. The handler doesn't need to see the pack to know what's going on by the change from long bawl mouth to hard chop.

Hounds make a lot of noise. This upsets some people, but hounds just do what they do, and I think its a beautiful thing. Raymond Graham once commented about one of my own hound's big mouth: "no sense shooting him; it'd just give him another hole to bark out of."

One day, as Ed was riding back to camp, he came across the carcass of a cow, not far from the river. She could've died from ticks, or calving, or who knows what. Ed, ever the opportunist, went back to camp to get the truck, drove back, and wiggled into where this old girl was. He hooked her up and drug the carcass down close to his hounds, for 'dog tucker'. Every day he'd ride by and knock some of that old cow off for his hounds.

Now Ed also had another dog, an Australian Shepherd he called Stubby. Stubby was Ed's cowdog, and he was a pretty good one. Stubby got to spend nights in the bunkhouse which was typical of working cowdogs. They pretty much lived with the cowboys.

Stubby had gotten into the routine of going for a trot on down to the river every day to 'dine' with the hounds. How could he resist that overpowering aroma of that old cow lying out in the sun for a week? No self-respecting dog could resist a temptation like that! None of us cowboys ever had a clue Stubby was disappearing every day to go down to dine with the boys, but after a while we sorta suspected it. It got to be where you couldn't help but notice, because Stubby was starting to get a little gassed up on this 'blue rare deli'.

The happy little fella would come trotting up to his ole 'Dad' and the rest of the crew, dancing around and breaking in half, happily passing gas to share with the rest of us. He even managed a grin for us as he wiggled around, with that funny bubble driving his insides crazy. AROMATIC??! Whew! Stubby was pretty hard to be around. That little black wiggly dog literally took our breath away! Ed would laugh and tell Stubby to 'get outside', then tell him 'good boy', for doing as he was told.

31

Now most nights, Stubby, from under Ed's bunk, and Rascal, from under Rock Creek's bunk, would get to grumbling at each other. One would growl, then the other one would growl, until they were told to shut up.

Well I guess one night, Stubby got tired of being told to shut up, and finally wanted to get his point across to Rascal. He'd just got plumb tired of arguing and came out from under Ed's bunk and started walking across the heaved old wood floor to Rock Creek's bunk.

I knew Ed and Rock Creek were still asleep because neither one of them had told the dogs to shut up yet. By this time, I was up on one elbow, waiting for the fight to get going; not that I could see much in the dark of that old bunkhouse. But I was sure wide awake, as there's no doubt there's going to be a donnybrook!

Click, click, click...Stubby's claws made the only sound in the bunkhouse. By the time he'd made it past the old 50 gallon drum we had for a wood stove, and half way to Rock Creek's bunk, Rascal had moved around to sit up, and was now silent, ready to meet Stubby head on.

I was up on the edge of my bunk now, waiting for the melee to get agoin'...but, absolute silence ensued...I waited...gurgling and sputtering sounds, not the savage flurry and snapping and growling of two tough cowdogs going at it like I was expecting!

Nope! It sounded like Stubby was vacating his bowels! Rock Creek must have gotten a snoot-full because he was the one to erupt into action, giving us a loud running commentary on the goings on!

Ed bounded up out of bed and got some light on the subject for us to see Rock Creek standing beside his bunk, pointing at a fast spreading substance on the floor, what had the appearance of green pea soup. Stubby had strategically laid his deposit on the floor directly in front of Rascal, which was right under Rock Creek's nose, by a distance of about 18 inches.

Poor Rock Creek had woken up to the full potency of Stubby's unsavoury bowel contents. Would been a heady challenge to the olfactory glands for sure.

There was Rock Creek, standing beside his bunk, still pointing at Stubby's deposit; with his shock of red hair, stark white cowboy hide, and blue gaunchies. He put me in the mind of the American flag, all red, white and blue!

32

Now Stubby was as happy as ever once again, doing his little break dance in the middle of the bunkhouse, until Ed quite graciously told Stubby "now get outside, good boy." Stubby bounded outside as Ed started looking around for an old saddle blanket or shirt, something to clean up Stubby's leavins; and John poked his head out from under twelve feather ticks and comforters to ask, "what's goin on?…" (John was a slim fella and needed a few more wraps and blankets than most).

Later, Rock Creek said to me, "Hey! First time I've ever heard a dog called "good boy" for messin' in the bunkhouse!"

Chapter Four
My New Hat

"If wisdom is not a benefit, after years of living, then there may be very few other riches."

I was thinking this morning about the new hat Possum got for me. I needed to get it over to Vern Elliot so he could punch a couple of eyelets in it. I wanted to attach a stampede string to it; which sure helps to keep it on my sloped forehead, especially when I get in a storm.

Thinking about my hat reminded me of Rock Creek, a fella I'd punched cows with over a lot of years, and a real good man to have with ya on a tough job. Him and his hat! It was always flying off his head, and that shock of red hair would be flying in the wind as him and his horse would be in hot pursuit of some critter or another…but that was Rock Creek. Seems like he'd get a chuckle at someone else's hat, and their 'whistle string', when their hat is still on their head and his has become part of the grassland somewhere, and most likely bent into a different shape, or else really stomped on. And, it would usually go back on his head that way, in open defiance to the general opinion of those riding with him…but, again, that was Rock Creek. He wouldn't be the one sitting there watching the work getting done with his hat on the back of his head trying to look punchy. Usually, he was the guy cutting the breeze, getting the job done. That's why I wondered what kept him from mounting a stampede string on his hat…defiance, I reckon.

Anyways, speaking of hats, one time I traded a hat off Mike Rose. We had a big cowboy trading session one weekend with Dwain Twan. I needed a new hat pretty bad, and couldn't afford one, so I was quick to jump on a trade for this hat when it came up. I didn't particularly care for the brown color, but it was made by American Hat Co., and they made some pretty good ones. Besides, a hat was a hat, to me at that time. It was a bit small for Mike, but it fit me fine; I could squash it down all right and keep it on my noggin in a chase. I shaped it up and started wearing it to work, and retired my old one with the big hole in the crown. I have to say, despite the color, I was real happy with my new hat.

Two weeks later, in early September, Dan (the Portland foreman) and I moved over to the Wilson Camp with Orval and some of the other hands from Dry Farm Camp. There was Jake Coutlee, Jerry McKenzie, Terry Milliken and Forty at the Wilson that year. Of course, everyone always wanted to go to the Wilson Camp and set their tents up in that pretty little meadow. It had a creek running through it, and was one of the nicest camps. We'd spend a week there gathering steers.

That particular year, Forty and I were the kids on the crew, and it was good to have a guy the same age as me to ride with for a change. Being young cowboys, stunts and dares became more frequent, and pretty soon, we were out to see whose horse was fastest, could stop the best, turn the best and even spook the best. But no horse Forty had could surpass my horse, Bullwinkle, for spook! He was well put together, a bay gelding, eight or nine years old, about 15.2 hands, and had lots of speed. But any little twig that snapped or piece of paper blowing in the wind, would get his eyes wide open and his rollers going.

I was riding Bullwinkle the day we trailed the yearling steers across Quilchena Creek valley to Dry Farm country. That was always a fun drive, trailing seven hundred steers across that pretty valley. Those steers sure lined out down the trail, as soon as we left the trap at the Wilson, and Orval and Jerry pointed them towards the old graveyard on the Hamilton Reserve. All the senior guys would ride up ahead along the swing and point, doing their level best to hold the herd down to a trot till we got to the valley floor. Usually by then, those big boys would settle down to a walk.

Then we'd snake them down to the old bridge by the old round corral and cross Quilchena Creek on the downstream side, and head on up the eastern slopes of the valley. Another couple of hours, and we'd drop the herd a mile or two from Dry Farm Camp. It sure was a good drive, getting those steers moved over, and we were ready for a good meal at the cookhouse.

Sharon was the cow camp cook at Dry Farm then, and she was one of the absolute best camp cooks around. She never disappointed us. It would be mouth-watering good, hot, and lots of it. A far cry from our own cowboy slum-gullion!

35

After we got done our lunch, we got on our horses, and started heading back to camp. We would be packing up and leaving the Wilson later that day after we got back. All that good dinner was settled in our bellies, and with the hot sun shining down on us in the middle of the day, we all started getting sleepy. So as we rode along, we started talking about things to while away the time, like guns, saddles, fast horses, silver bits and hats.

Forty peered at my head and asked to have a look at my new hat. I handed it over to him, and he tried it on, admired it, figured I'd made a good trade, and started to pass it back to me.

Now, it would be hard to imagine that a horse would have been asleep the whole while we were passing this hat back and forth, but one had to remember I was riding Bullwinkle, and Bullwinkle had the ability to completely detach himself from the proceedings, and nod off. And he had the propensity to come back to life at the most unexpected and inopportune times—throwing himself and everyone else around him into a real commotion, and probably not fully aware of where he even was.

Of course, now was the time for Bullwinkle to come back from the 'land of nod', just as I was taking my hat back from Forty. I had my right hand hung out there with that big brown hat, and suddenly Bullwinkle's eyes rolled back, he let out a big snort and was already in a flat spin! I was used to these kind of sprees, but Forty was right excited about our little performance, and yelled at me "I didn't know he could turn like that!" "Aw, this ain't nuthin…" I says, acting like this wasn't even half throttle. "Watch him go now!"

I stuck that hat down to within 18 inches of his right eye, and we darn near stopped the earth from turning! That's a lot of fun for the first three turns, but then all the blood rushes to your eyeballs, and you can't see so good…By then, my arm was stuck straight out to the side at a 90 degree angle from the horse, and I was having a real hard time getting back in the middle of Bullwinkle. Think it can't happen? You mix an athletic horse with a dinosaur brain, coupled with a really high level of self-preservation instinct, and a young cowboy with 30 lbs of meat in his belly, and I tell you, it can!

Forty started hollering at me through the din and blur of things. "Drop the hat! Drop the hat!! Drop. The. Hat!!" Only one thought was running through my bluntly awakened mind, "DON'T drop the hat! Not my NEW hat!"

Another flat turn, and it was pretty obvious to me, it was the thing to do, and drop the hat I did. Of course, now Bullwinkle can't really remember why he was even spooking, but he did another three or four real nice turns, just because, and all of them right on top of my hat! Well, he finally coasted into a nice landing again on Mother Earth and I got off and stood unsteadily on my two pegs looking down at my crushed hat. He'd managed to put a foot right in the crown. It wasn't cut, there was no hole in it, which I was real thankful for, but it forever after had a bad crease halfway up the crown. A cheap lesson, after all; but at least it had provided good entertainment for the entire crew.

Before long, we got back to the Wilson and rolled our bedrolls and threw them in the truck. Forty and I left the guys to finish loading the rest of the camp, and we changed horses to wrangle the cavvy back to Dry Farm. It was late afternoon as we crossed Quilchena Creek, and got the horses settled into a walk and up the east side of the valley.

I looked around me at all the hills of bunchgrass as far as the eye could see, and was a tired but happy cowboy…Although, I was kind of wishing I would've kept my hat on my head.

Chapter Five
Forty and Deefer

"It takes about three years to get to know your home range; how to think ahead of your herd, be able to do your day's work and still have horseflesh left over for the ride home. I wholeheartedly believe this, as do most experienced hands. And, in rough country, where a cowboy might be a bit short handed, or in the heavy timber, a good dog can sure help save the day."

Jerry McKenzie mentioned one time a fella should know how to cowboy first before using a dog to do the job. And Mario Corriveau told me once he reckoned there was more fights started amongst cowboys over a dog than maybe any other reason. Maybe he was right.

Sometimes those dogs do get to scrapping, quite often due to territorial issues, maybe ignored or not dealt with by the handler, which in turn causes hard feelings amongst the crew. But for the most part, our cowdogs want to help us and we get to really appreciate them, trouble or not. They help lots, and in the long run, create fodder for many stories.

If you have ever heard the statement that a dog takes on his master's traits, believe it. The hard, long days and situations that are tough to deal with really bring the cowboy's (or cowgirl's) characters to the surface. No different for their pardners, the horse and the dog. They all get to a point where a cow doesn't dare step out of line on the trail before a dog has got the jump on her, lest he has to use up a lot of energy bringing her back from a greater distance. And if the dog isn't there, then the horse gets wise and goes after that cow with ears back as soon as she heads off the trail.

But the dog really watches his handler; that's his pardner. And they even develop certain personality traits akin to him. Sometimes they act very much like the cowboy.

Like Forty. He got that nickname because he said he was from Earl Grey, Saskatchewan, and upon being asked where that was, replied "forty miles from Regina". Everyone had a nickname, and nobody took exception to it. Him and his brother Neil got to be real good hands at whatever they did. And to say Forty was off the cuff is an understatement. You never knew what he was going to come up with or what statements would come out of his mouth.

He had a dog that was, well, I guess he was a Heinz 57. Don't know what he was, but he had lots of hair. You could see his eyes, but he had lots of hair. And just the same as Forty, was happy go lucky and never wanting to miss anything. I never saw him take of dip of snoose, but I did hear him swear a time or two, so I guess Forty managed to teach him something...Forty called him 'Deefer'...'D fer dog.'

It just seemed to me that Deefer was born to be with Forty. Not that Forty was ugly because them Edenoste boys weren't homely fellas, but him and that dog were sure geared the same.

If there was nothing going on, Deefer just found something to do, right or wrong, and he did it big. More than once, Orval, our foreman at Douglas Lake Cattle Company, got right choked about Deefer wrangling horses at night. Course, them cowdogs gotta do things. If they were a lap dog they wouldn't be any good on a cow outfit.

Forty told me a story one time that puts me in mind of just how well them two knew each other. Forty was still back at Douglas Lake then, and was calving cows down at the Morton camp. This was 1986 as I recall. He'd driven down to the Home Ranch one night to visit his wife, and next morning he was rushing around to get going to work and Deefer was nowhere to be seen. Normally Deefer would have known by his own clock that it was time to be in the back of the truck, but I guess he had more pressing matters to attend to.

Anyhow, Forty couldn't wait any longer, so he left. Deefer must have seen the truck leaving and lit out right behind him in hot pursuit, and ran all the way up to Minnie Lake Ranch, instead of the Morton. Minnie Lake was another camp belonging to Douglas Lake, where Forty had calved cows the spring before. It was about 15 miles from Douglas Lake's Home Ranch.

Helmut Gawhens, the cowboy at Minnie Lake, saw ole Deefer come galloping through the yard, looking here and there for Forty's truck. Not seeing it, he galloped on. The last time Helmut saw Deefer, he was lined out on a hard run in a beeline across the hills in the direction of the Morton camp, having figured out that must be where his pardner was. Which, as the crow flies, would have been another ten miles from Minnie Lake.

Now all this is unbeknownst to Forty, who had by this time arrived at the Morton, caught up and saddled Hugo for the day, and crammed some eggs down his gullet. He then lined out across the Howse Field, across the road from the Morton, making a big circle through a bunch of cows scattered around there to calve out.

Forty and Hugo were pickin' 'em up and puttin' 'em down across Howse Field when he spotted a coyote way up ahead crossing a little valley by Muskrat Lake. The reason it really attracted his attention was the way it was travelling along. It wasn't just moochin' along following its nose looking for a mouse or something; it was really honed in on something and sure covering country! Furthermore, he figured it was much too black for a coyote and too big as well; could be he was watching a wolf. Forty had it in his mind that it was after something, maybe a calf, so he pointed ole Hugo's ears in that direction and took off, to see what that critter was up to.

As he got closer, Forty's pretty sure it is a wolf because of its colour and the way its stretched out and travelling. This was getting exciting for him, so down comes his string. He wants to see if he can dab a loop on this wolf before he gets to a calf. A little fun with a calf killer to liven up a cowboy's day is just not to be passed up!

Forty bumped ole' Hugo into high gear and Hugo was glad to oblige. He had his neck stretched out and ears back like he'd been chasin' wolves all his life! Johnny Wolf saw that horse and rider bearing down and him and he found high gear too! Once he heard the thunder of those hooves pounding closer to him, he stretched that long black body out and was close to the ground and tail streaming out behind.

Forty and Hugo closed the gap in short order, and pretty soon Johnny Wolf is ducking this way and ducking that way, doing everything he can do to evade those thundering hooves; but Hugo stuck to him like a fly in the jam. Forty was getting ready to throw a nice little calf loop and snag him the same time as Mr. Wolf threw a quick, traumatized look back over his shoulder, and son of a gun! Forty recognized Deefer.

Well, it took him a bit to rein in Hugo because the horse was enjoying this entertainment, a lot; and it was all Forty could do to stay in the saddle from laughing so hard.

He said Deefer seemed quite happy this little exercise was over, but I reckon he was wondering why he ever became a cowdog, only to be left at home, run 30 miles to work and then provide sordid entertainment to his good pardner to boot!

Chapter Six
Our Musical Cowboss

"One person's perspective may be less about how they think and more about where they have been."

My pardner, Jason Coutlee, and I were riding a couple of four year-olds one day. It was their first day out to work. Orval had hauled the cowboy crew up to White Lake, Quilchena Cattle Company's yearling range. Orval was the cowboss at Quilchena at that time. He wanted to gather up our dry cows and ship them, but they were scattered throughout the heifer pasture, and he thought there were some out on the Lauder Ranch side of the fence too. So he sent Jason and I off on our own to ride the Lauder range to see if we could locate those dry cows. It would be a good circle for our colts, once we got them talked into lining straight out instead of zig-zagging back and forth trying to get back to their buddies.

Orval and the rest of the crew were starting to line out up the hill to start a gather in the heifer pasture, and I told Jason that maybe we should find out from Orval how many dries we were looking for. Orval turned his horse around and looked at me when I asked that, and he thought for a second, trying to recall how many he'd seen, and then responded, "La La La La 'Leven" Orval had a slight stutter that only came out once in a while, and this was one of those times.

As Jason and I rode away, gee-hawing our colts back and forth, doing our level best to keep them in a straight line, I said to Jason, "See, our pardner was trying to cheer us up good by striking up a little tune—La La La La."

We had a real chuckle over that; I remember Jason wiping his eyes, laughing...We'd recall that moment from time to time, as the years passed, and always got a good chuckle out of it. It wasn't that we laughed at Orval, or disrespected him in any way, because we all had so much respect for him. He was one of the best stockmen around and was an incredibly organized boss. Many top hands learned a lot from Orval.

But in our lifestyle, you laughed at a lot of things most other folks would see as offensive. Every opportunity to laugh was

welcome, 'cause the days were long, maybe real hot or real cold, maybe raining or snowing, or maybe you'd be riding a horse you didn't get along with; so laughter makes it all better.

I've noticed that a lot of the folks I've worked around, that have had some hard times, were usually more prone to laugh at a situation that might have offended someone else. Also, years later, when you try to recall a person's face, it's always easier to recall those faces that were full of laughter, smiling. And Jason was one of those people. When you recall him, his smiling face comes instantly to mind.

Chapter Seven
Spook's Bear Story

"If you can learn more about empathy by visiting another person's situation, then why couldn't you do that for a dog, horse, or cow?"

I was walking a fence line back around the House Field a few days ago and saw fresh bear sign on the trail by the fence. It got me to thinking about, "What if I was one of those guys who had a dog that ran into that bear, and then brought it back to me, looking for protection?" Then I was reminded of the time my horse, Duster, waited for me to get up from my snooze to get away from a big brown bear.

I was riding for Douglas Lake at the time, and I had a nice five year-old bay gelding named Duster. That day, Dan Stocking and I were up in the Gilmore pastures moving yearling steers up higher. I'd finished my circle and got to the little water hole where Dan and I had agreed to meet up, but Dan wasn't there yet. It was a foggy morning, but the sun was breaking through, and it felt nice and warm, and I started getting sleepy. So, I stepped down off Duster and wrapped the reins around my wrist and lay down to check my eyelids for cracks for a few minutes.

I must have just nodded off when Duster woke me up rattling his nose, snorting and touching my leg with his nose. I looked up at him and his ears were straight ahead, his head way up and looking down the hill; something was sure bothering him. Then he'd look down at me again, bump my leg, and throw his head up high again.

I sat up and looked around, and there was a big brown bear grazing across the hillside right towards us, no more than 50 yards away. I came wide-eyed off the ground so fast I made Duster jump back, but he waited for this slow poke to get in the saddle before he bolted out of there!

'Course, then I was reminded of ole Spook McCrae, who was telling me a funny story one time about dogs and bears. Spook was a real good cowboy, from Spahomin Reserve, by Douglas Lake. Like so many of the native cowboys from that valley, he had a lot of natural *sabe* and was a real smooth hand. He was always cheerful, a real gentleman and invariably had a good story to while away those long rides home. I learned a lot from him.

I think Spook and Jerry Matheson were getting some fences ready up Portland range way, for Douglas Lake, and it must have been an ugly piece of fence, because they were walking it out, having left the horses at home for this one. Jerry had a little collie dog that would wander on up ahead and come back once in a while to check out the boys. Then it would trot on up ahead, sniffing here and there, like dogs do when they're reading the newspaper.

That little dog had been gone for a while when they heard it barking like hell and they figured it must have run onto a bear. That was the first thought in their minds, so they looked around for some place to save themselves, and the closest thing to them was a big old stump of a tree, about two feet in diameter and around 3 feet tall. It sounded like the dog was getting close, and they figured they didn't have a lot of time before the dog and Mr. Bear would be underfoot, so they got behind that stump, just in time to see Jerry's dog come down that fence line with his back legs passing his front ones, looking to get a little help from 'Dad', with his tail between his legs, and Mr. Bear right behind him! The bear was a brown-coloured black bear, and only an average size, as black bears go—which is plenty big when they're breathing on your tail!

Jerry and Spook both climbed for the top of the stump, but there's only room for one and they collided, and down comes Jerry, just as his dog and his new playmate come around the stump! Up the stump goes Jerry again, and down goes Spook. They both took their turns on the stump, never once managing to both stay up there. This went on for a couple minutes; long enough to play them both out, jumping up on that stump, and the whole time Jerry's yelling at his dog to "get outside!" (a phrase cowboys use to get their dogs to leave the herd and lay down someplace else while sorting, or the like, is being done.)

Finally Jerry's message got through to his dog, and he 'got outside'; running off down the fence again, taking the bear with it, until they came across a bear cub. And that's where the dog finally got relief from the chase.

Spook said he didn't think that bear was even aware of the cowboys, so intent was he on catching the dog! It turns out the bear was a Mrs. Bear, with a cub, and Spook said they sure kept a close eye on where that dog went after that! "GEE, we was played out" Spook said.

Chapter Eight
Freedom and Dignity

"When I think of the tough times we all go through in life, and the hurdles we wrestle with; I reflect on people, cowboys and critters I have known that meet their day to day struggles with a cheerful outlook and a job to do. And in 'most all cases, I'm left with the following perspective, strengthened a little more, each time I witness their resolve:

When the body is strong but the spirit is broken, it is difficult to go on. But, if the body is broken, and the spirit strong, you will endure"

I knew a little old black cow when I was riding at the Gang Ranch, that really brought that message home to me, at a time when I most needed it...and remember, there are no coincidences...She had a Circle S brand on her ribs, a cow that had been one of a load of cows purchased from ole Lyle James years before, to help build up the cow herd numbers. She was one of the only ones of these cows left, a smaller cow, built pretty close to the ground, and she was starting to get a little long in the tooth (if she had any left that last year). She had a hitch in her get-along, an injury or fall, I suppose, to one of her hips which left her with that 'arthur' (arthritis) quite a few of us become acquainted with.

It's hard not to notice a cow like this, in the midst of a herd of younger cows with good conformation. But when she really caught my eye was one day around the end of June, as we were building herds and trailing them through the old Home Ranch Valley. That's where we'd be starting our turnout to the mountain country.

Me and the crew had a big herd thrown together, about 300 pair, and were walking them up the road for Home Ranch Valley. I had Nolan and Ken up on the point, cowboys who knew the trail and where to stop the herd. I was back on the drag with the rest of the crew making sure all those babies followed along. We never had a lot of calves on the drag on this drive, as the cows were paired up pretty well before we trailed out. On some drives, there's lots of calves that drop back to the drag, looking for their mammas, and life can get real interesting; a cowboy won't have much time to look at anything else but calves. But not so on this drive.

I noticed our little black Circle S cow had dropped back to the drag with her own baby beside her, fairly soon after leaving the rodear grounds. Her calf was a pretty nice little calf. I mean, of a size already that you could say he'd probably be near half her weight come weaning time. And she wasn't losing sight of her pride and joy. She was limping along on her bad hip, in the midst of about 30 calves, and I told the boys to just drop her back. She could stay in the pasture that we were trailing across.

There was a nice little stream there, and with all the other cows gone for the rest of the summer, there'd be plenty of grass, and no reason for her to walk more than she really needed to. But none of us took into consideration how much that little cow figured she 'needed' to travel. We cut her back away from the herd, and had to work at that, as she seemed determined to travel along. Finally she stopped, gave us cowboys a hard look, and turned her nose up a cow trail through a meadow we were passing that paralleled the road. She limped away, with her calf following along, up the side of the herd till she was about a hundred yards ahead of us. Before she popped back into the herd, she gave us one more hard look, as if we'd sure enough offended her by making her go through all that work just to fall back in with the herd again! Cowboys! We got a chuckle out of that.

One sure had to admire that stubborn little cow; she was coming along, and THAT was THAT. Within another couple of miles, we reached the Home Ranch Valley corrals, and she hadn't dropped back to the drag. So, when we held up the herd to part off dries and cripples into the pasture there, to await the dry cow gather at the end of July, we had to really look for the old girl. I spotted her, and sorted her out of the herd once again, and, together with her calf, walked them through the slipwire with the bunch of dry cows. She went along with my idea well enough that time; I suppose in part because she needed to have a rest anyway, but I remember well the look she gave me as we left her there and shut the slipwire gate...

yup, she looked offended.

Those long days of trailing cows up to the mountains turned to weeks, and as they say, "time flies when you're having fun". We got most of the herds moved around how we wanted them, and about the end of July it was time to leave a couple of hands up in the mountains there to care for those cattle. The rest of us moved back down to Home Ranch Valley to gather the dries up for the dry cow sale.

After a day settling into camp, we rode out the next morning to bunch up dries and sort them into the corral for shipping. The odd lame animal would stay there for the summer, so although we looked for our little black Circle S cow, we never saw her. We even had a re-ride, along the creek, in case she brushed up in the willows, but no, she wasn't there. Well, work must go on, so we put her in the back of our minds; but it was odd that our cow count of all the stock we'd left there would be right on, and yet we had that one cripple cow missing and her pride and joy calf.

We figured it wasn't impossible that she'd wandered off and laid down one last time, under the trees somewhere, but we thought we'd of seen her calf somewhere. With other jobs to turn our hands to, there wasn't a lot of time to spend looking around for one pair, so we moved on.

Those summer days passed by with all the cows to move, colts to start, and before long, fall works were looking at us again. Those pretty days when the mornings are pleasantly cool and the air is so clear up in those hills that you can hear a cow bawl for her calf from miles away, and you'd swear she's lots closer...It was mid-October, the leaves were falling off the trees, and we were gathering cattle down from the mountains to wean calves off them at our Fosberry camp.

The weather was nice enough that those girls weren't ready to come down from their favourite spots yet. Rule of thumb with cowboys in this country is: if the 'White Cowboy' comes down on us through the night, those cattle will give their backs a shake next morning as they walk out from under a tree, and they'll head down to lower spots on their own, or most of them will. But, if the weather stays nice, and it's great riding, plan on doing lots because cowboys will have to cover a lot of country to convince those cows it's time to head home…

One Sunday, I had given the crew a long weekend to blow off steam in Williams Lake before we got in the thick of weaning season. My ole pardner Merv and I decided we'd take a ride up to a camp along a chain of meadows, called Big Meadow, which was a couple hours ride from Fosberry Camp. We were short for our first weaning by a couple hundred head. Larry, the manager, was coming up in a couple of days to help us scale calves and load them on trucks. He'd spent a lot of time getting the scale set up at the Fosberry corrals, and had trucks ordered, so it sure wouldn't do to have a short weaning after all that planning. Merv and I figured Big Meadow would have a few more cattle straggled in that country, even though we'd covered those meadows the week before.

After a good breakfast early Sunday morning, we jogged out of camp. The horses were feeling good and fresh, as we'd just changed up our strings a week or two beforehand. Rollers going in the bits and spurs ringing, the horses were eager to move out. It sure was a pretty day. By the time we reached Big Swamp, our horses had a good sweat going after the long climb. Big Swamp was the first meadow to ride across, and we were happily surprised to see a fair few head of cattle had straggled in. No surprise, really, I thought, as there was snow up in the peaks already.

By the time we had gathered Big Meadow and Big Swamp, we were happy to see we had over 150 pairs to take down the trail with us. Those ole girls had full bellies and moved out easily for us. Merv took a good jag for a point down the trail to Fosberry meadow, while Tomcat (my mount) and my little collie dog Polly and I brought up the drag. I was sure happy; a pretty day, a good horse between my knees, a good dog and a guy who knew the job and the trail up on the point. It looked like this week's weaning was going to go alright after all.

The trail from Big Swamp back down to Fosberry Meadows is a trail cut through the timber, and quite a bit of it narrows down to only about 15 feet wide. So it takes a while to get your drag started down there, as those cows need a little time to look around for their calf, before pointing their nose forward and taking the trail. Generally, them stronger cows get a going up ahead, and before long, any older stock, heavier, lame ones, will end up right on the

51

drag. I guess I hadn't followed the drag more than half an hour's walk down the trail when who shows up right in front of me? That little circle S cow and her calf, who is not so little now, but a nice, fat steer calf, about 550 lbs! I just stopped my horse dead in his tracks for a moment thought "naw, it couldn't be"…but sure enough, there was no mistaking that bad hip and the way she shuffled along. Only now, the poor old girl looked a little rougher, and the hitch-in-her-gitalong was a bit worse and I said so right out loud, I guess as much to myself as to my horse and dog.

I suppose a guy gets to thinking out loud like that to his pardners…At the sound of my voice, she stopped her shuffling and looked back at me with that same 'fire in her eye'. Then, she looked at her calf and spoke to him, "mm", and started her shuffling along again. I told her "yes, he is a nice calf, and you did a good job, little mama", and let her pick the pace. By the time we got to the meadows where Merv had turned the point loose to graze, I was quite a ways behind with the drag. In fact, Merv was starting to wonder if he shouldn't come back down the trail looking for me. Then he heard me talking to my pardners, and out of the timber and into the meadow shuffles our long lost Circle S cow. He was as surprised as I had been. We left the herd there, and as they spread out to graze, the fat calves laid down. Merv and I rode home real pleased with how our day had worked out.

Days of weaning, shipping calves, and preg checking the cow herd rolled on by pretty quick. It seems you spend a lot of time roping out your horses for the next day at last light. We had a full weaning that week as I recall. We were a little over 600 head; a good gather for nice weather like we were having. We got our cows preg checked and were happy with the results. I looked at the herd of cows we were trailing from the corrals at Fosberry, back up to Kane Meadow where the girls could happily put their faces back in the fall grass, and I thought about our little Circle S cow.

In fact, I thought about her a lot, and I mentioned to the crew we should maybe just split up on our ride back to camp and keep an eye open for her. Sure enough, one of the guys soon gave out a yell and we went and had a last look at her. She had laid down one last time under her beloved jack pine trees, facing the mountains she loved to spend the summer in.

That place in her mind where she needed to go, with that crippled little body: her favourite meadow, I suppose, not too far from a stream; a good place to raise her calf. And she had laid down where she wanted to.

Knowing that little cow brought a lot of things home to me. She lived and died, with a lot of freedom, and dignity. As choked up as us humans can get over a thing like that—the cow, the horse; they are so adaptable. And as I rode into camp, and saw smoke curling from the cookhouse stove pipe, I felt a lot wiser, and healthier inside about second guessing myself when it comes to jobs like weaning those calves off their moms…it's a job that needs to be done, and it is what it is. I have the freedom to treat all God's critters with the same respect and dignity which I saw in that little Circle S cow.

53

Chapter Nine
A Night With Orval and Petunia

"When I am feeling pain, I stop and consider someone else's; the very act of thinking about someone else's anguish eases the ache inside of me.....Empathy is truly one of the greatest emotional processes that I have nurtured."

Possum has a saying that she used a lot when leading tours; one I like and use myself now. "Everybody's got a story". Most everyone knows this but I find I think about it more as I get older. A quick and simple enough thought; but one that really packs a punch to me now. I battled cancer for a couple of years, and like a lot of people who go through it, many less fortunate than I; I found myself a bit weaker than I had been and a bit more lonely than I had been before.

Lonesome, even in a crowd. You think nobody sees or cares, but somewhere in the crowd, someone, maybe several someones are watching. Maybe not with their eyes, but they're watching. It may be a case of somebody you know giving the impression that they're avoiding you. But I know something different now; they are uncomfortable. They are so overwhelmed with the complexity of your own situation that any words they may conjure seem inadequate to them. They are not yet at a place in their life where they realize this factor, whatever they say DOES create the impression that they care. It's a God given gift that we all have; we care. About something...

I had taken a cowboying job at Quilchena Cattle Company at a time when I really did not want to carry the weight of a boss's job. I just wanted to go places ahorseback. So, when Orval Roulston offered me a job at Quilchena, I took it. I thought it's time to put the mind to rest and just stay on a horse.

I was glad for other reasons as well. I knew the Rose family that owned the outfit, liked them, and was comfortable around them. Great spring and summer range to ride, a cavvy of big travelling geldings to put in front of a cow and see the country with, and a good crew to work with. So, it seems, all things considered, my security blanket was well in place. Time to heal. I had worked for Orval 15 years prior to this time and, like the rest of the crew, found him to be a well-organized boss. He liked animals, and when you showed up for work, it was done right, or don't bother showing up. When you worked for Orval, you knew you had put in a full day. We all sure learned a lot from him.

Quilchena was quite an outfit to cowboy at. You were always riding; always working cows and looking at cow country. I was to put in 15 wonderful years there, eventually cowboying with Possum and riding with both my daughters, Emily and Shannon.

Now, Orval had a voice that was more like a soft growl, best way I can describe it; from an old injury to his throat. To top that off, he had a slight stutter when he talked. At least, until he was upset. Then it came out loud and clear! Orval really liked to get people's attention if need be; that way, he said he didn't have to chew that cabbage twice.

But for the most part, a fella really had to listen close when Orval was divvying out everyone's circle. Especially me. I don't wear these marvellous contraptions of German engineering in my ears because I have such acute hearing. The only thing 'acute' about it all is I find that people say more odd and amusing statements now than they did before I needed these gadgets…

Well, I made it through spring works, and we got the herds turned out to the high country in early summer. About that time I started getting a bit weaker from my condition. Orval took me aside one day and told me I should oughta move over from the bunkhouse to his cabin, as there was an extra bunk in there, and I'd likely get more rest. He reckoned that them young fellas might want to sit up at night and regale each other with tales of daring, but knowing I needed my rest, they couldn't carry on like they wanted to. Orval said his log cabin was nice and quiet and a good place to rest.

So, that's what I did. I moved my bedroll and kit over to his place. There I had a bunk in the corner of the one room cabin; this room being partially divided in the middle by a tall set of wooden shelves. The only other fixtures in the room were a couple of gun racks, a table, wood stove and a pressure tank for the water system. Yes we had running water; and we even had electric lights.

I recall my first evening in that place. Nice and cool, and a relief from the heat outside. When I laid down to rest, I had to cover over to warm up again. Back in the bunkhouse, a singlewide trailer which doubled as the cookhouse, the crew spent their wakeful nights wishing they could bring their dog in to wag his tail in their face like a fan. The cowboys lovingly referred to the old trailer as the 'sardine tin'.

I think that's why Mike Rose got it in his head to build Orval's log cabin, and eventually a nice cookhouse a few years later. Mike and Tracy Charters built that cabin, and what a comfortable retreat it came to be; in all kinds of weather. In the cool fall days it was sure a pleasure to come into from bad weather and fire up that wood stove, which was made from a 50 gallon barrel. We had to be careful not to stoke her up too much though, and get her to dancin' in one spot. That stove would heat things up in a hurry. Even the flies would be crawling out of the cracks in the logs with their tongues a-hangin' out.

Well, back to my first night in there. I have a tough time nodding off to sleep in a new place, at least for a couple of nights anyway. I guess I can say it, I had a few reasons to like to have my eyes open anyway. But Orval seemed to be paying a bit of attention to the fact that there was a guest in his cabin and he wanted him to rest.

Now Orval was attached. He had a little Cocker Spaniel female whose name was Petunia. A real friendly little dog. "Tunie" went everywhere with Orval, even on a lot of his rides. And she seemed to like Miles all right, because when we were piled in the company truck heading to camp, or just going to put out salt blocks, Miles let her sit in his lap. It was an easier reach for her little head to look out the window and get the breeze.

So of course it was a real novelty for Tunie to have Miles come and live with her as well, and she'd come over to my side of the cabin to visit. Orval would call her back, and I'd hear him mumbling to her "na na now, Tunie, you leave him alone", and I could just imagine him giving her little head a pat and smiling at her. You see, in those days, my ears could hear a bit better than they do now.

Night time rolled around, and we read books for a while before shutting the light out and hitting the hay.

I eventually dropped off to sleep, but then, in the middle of the night, I woke up to the sound of Orval flashing up a smoke. Did I mention that Orval smoked? Enough that he needed to complete his daily quota by having one or two smoke breaks at night…good for the mind, you know? It gets a fella thinking. Remember the old saying "a smoking man is a thinking man"? I had a pipe box that had that saying on it.

Anyways, I could hear Orval hauling away on that cigarette, sitting over there in the dark. About 3 good drags, and she was all done. Then came hacking time; I'd been around him a lot and I know it's coming. Yup, he starts to cough, but wants to stifle it, and I can hear him get to his feet and start to scurry for the door! Now, once outside he cuts loose and really does his level best to cough up a lung. I reckon it must have been the fresh air; he sure didn't cough that bad inside…Raw air can be tough on a person!

Well, after he'd exercised his belly muscles enough by getting rid of that fresh air, he decided that was good enough for him. I could hear the door open, then close, and soft tippy toe steps back to his bunk. I laid there throughout this session of self-preservation, the entire time with my back to the room, giving my level best impression of a possum playing dead (pardon the pun, Possum).

In my mind, I figured business would now slow down, but I guess little Tunie was wide awake by this time and figured she needed a midnight snack. She must have had a few crumbles of dog food in her dish yet that the mice had not helped themselves to. Orval kept her dish across the room by her water bowl and the water tap. So, across the room goes Tunie, click click click click, across the wooden floor. Grab one crumble, click click click click, back to her rug by the bed. No self-respecting Cocker Spaniel drools and slobbers into her food bowl like any common hound. Tunie was a real little lady.

Crunch crunch crunch crunch…back to the dish, click click click click; one more crumble and back to the rug; crunch crunch crunch crunch…at this point, Orval found it necessary to rein her in a bit and I could hear him admonish her "na na now Tunie…you're gonna wake him up!" You see, everyday human noises, like uncontrollable coughing, will lull the human to sleep,

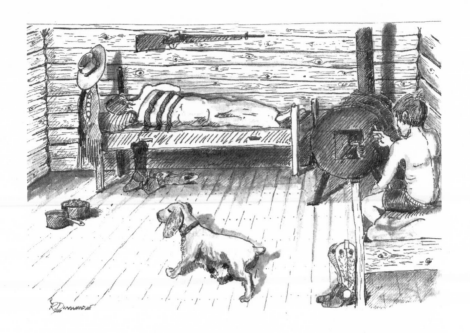

whereas a dog eating crumbles could cause a cowboy to wake up!!

In hindsight, we think we know a person after spending a fair amount of time with them, and really just don't pay close attention anymore, until one day, maybe years later, reflection helps us to see where their heart really was.

Chapter Ten
Polly and The Sow Griz

"I'm so glad I have had such a big backyard for me, my horses and dogs to roam in all these years. As a result of this freedom, there has been even less of a reason to keep track of the hours of work, or days of rest."

During the summer of '98 there were a lot of forest fires in BC. It would be hard to forget that summer's raging fires. Most fires don't affect a lot of people, but once in a while you'll see on the news or hear tell of a town evacuated; people taking what they could scoop, and driving away.

That summer I was working for Quilchena Cattle Company, breaking colts and building a new set of round corrals at the Triangle Ranch. We'd heard about the fire on Thynne Mountain, high up on the ranch's summer range, and never realized, like most people, that it would rage out of control overnight. It became one of those fires that had people in the Otter Valley evacuating homes; cowboys, loggers and farmers throwing together and hauling families' hastily packed belongings away in horse trailers, pickups, and cars.

We were getting reports that the fire, fed by winds, was arcing across watersheds, and sparks igniting new fires as much as a half mile away. Before that fire was eventually extinguished, it had destroyed some 11,000 hectares (27,000 acres) of forest, but fortunately no homes.

The range this fire destroyed was right in the heart of cattle range used by Quilchena Cattle Company and Nicola Ranch. During that time of evacuation of the Bar O Bar Ranch, and neighbouring ranches in the area, cowboys were deployed within what we considered a safe working distance of the fire, to gather any cattle left behind, and move them down range, to prevent them getting trapped by the fire. (Something the fire fighters have not allowed since.)

Well, I don't recall that we ran into a whole lot of cows, but there were some hanging around that needed chousing down the hill. Orval Raulston and I were straggling the McPhail creek country and decided we'd just split up for a bit and each cut a different circle, then meet up a ways down McPhail creek before we headed down to the truck and trailer. With a fire like that one, you sure had to be careful splitting up like that, but we both knew the country pretty well, and we were over the ridge from the fire.

I'd travelled for about an hour and came to a cut block with quite a few young trees growing in it, most of them about 12-15 feet high. It was pretty close together in places. I got up on top of a little knob, my horse, my dog and I, and sat, looking down towards the bottom end of the cut block. My horse needed a breather anyway, so I thought that'd be a good time to have a look around…that's one thing a cowboy likes to do; get up somewhere high and look around.

Something moved down there, about a half mile away, and it was kind of hard to get a good look at it, but by the height of its back and the reddish colour, it was a cow, all right, and then I saw its calf moving between those young trees. We'd rested long enough and I decided to head on down to pick the old girl up.

It took us a while to pick our way through some of that blow down and slash, and by the time we'd reached the spot I'd marked where I'd seen the cow go in, she could've been anywhere. I sent my dog Polly in there to pick up a trail so I'd know where that old cow was.

Obviously, she hadn't gone too far with her baby after all, because I could hear Polly open up right away and Polly never did say anything unless she was face to face at work with a cow. But by the sound of things, Polly was having a tough time of it, so I pointed my horse's nose towards her and headed on in to help, bumping my knees from tree to tree.

I don't reckon I went more than a hundred yards before I was getting close to Polly, and just before I got to her, I caught a look at something moving fast to my right, then something moving fast a little further in; suddenly the whole patch of bush was alive! Everything was happening real fast in there, and I stopped to take stock of the situation. Just then, I saw a third critter as it crossed a small clearing, and in that brief glimpse, I saw enough to make my senses come alive!

What I'd just seen was a yearling griz! He had a stripe across his withers, maybe silver coloured, maybe buckskin? But there were three of them busting brush out of there pronto, and Polly was still working hard, less than 100 feet ahead of me. My horse wasn't taking another step in that direction, and by now I knew my little dog was working a sow griz, and it went through my mind that poor little Polly had never had anything to do with bears before! Especially at those close quarter, and if I didn't get her out of there quick, she'd be just a burp!

I spurred my mare hard and busted into another small clearing, maybe an old landing, and there they were; that big old sow and Polly running circles around in there, and I mean fast! I don't know how that little dog stayed away from that nasty old girl, cause she was really moving. I gave a few loud yells, and I couldn't hold my horse there any longer, but it was enough; as my horse plunged her way through and over, and anything but around the trees, I cast a quick glance over my shoulder and got an eyeful of Polly coming; back feet passing her front ones, and that big old griz with that massive head breathing up Polly's backside!

I'll never forget that picture. It's amazing how you can see so much in such a short time, and even more amazing how long that picture is etched in your mind, when things get busy like that! It was the last thing I saw till I was out of the brush.

I stopped and looked around for Polly; she was already coming up beside me, and as she went past, I'll always remember another picture: that look she gave me...because it said "where in hell were ya? I could've used ya back there!" That look spoke louder than words and it was no doubt that's what she was thinking.

I reckon that old sow forgot about us pretty quick, and went after her young ones, because she hadn't chased us too far. But I still can't be too sure how far we cut the breeze, cause heartbeats were minutes and yards mere inches!

Chapter Eleven
My Camp Cooking "Surprize Stew"

"A fella can squawk all he wants about cooking, but the proof is in the puddin' when he has to buckle down and do it himself!"

Now many's the time a cowboy will need to cook for himself, up in a lonely camp; whether it be out under a fir tree, or up in a cabin. But the only ones who have to put up with the taste are himself and his dog. When it comes to cooking for someone else, the pressure is on, cause you don't want to have to listen to any whining and complaining, on top of having to be the chef. After a spell, a fella can get kind of cranky with trying to please hungry cowboys after riding hard all day himself. Then a guy gets to where you don't even care what it tastes like, and maybe even just waits for someone to say something is wrong with the grub.

When I was running Empire Valley Ranch, we all had plenty of opportunity to practice our culinary skills over a campfire. Tex, Ivan, Cory, Chona, Cliff and I were trying to gather all our cows up along the breaks of the Fraser river in April, and it was taking some hard rides to come up with a handful of cows and calves every day.

I was talking to my good buddy, Tim O'Byrne one day, who was cowboss over at the Gang Ranch across Churn Creek. He volunteered to bring his whole crew over and set up camp with us; that way, given a couple weeks of gathering and parting off dries and late calvers, we could plan one big brand. That would free up me and the boys and my oldest son Jesse to just spend our days throwing a big herd together.

We had a good sized pasture with water and feed to hold the herd, and there was a real old cabin adjacent to it that had a little creek running past it, to use as a camp. So we set to work and built a Russell fence around it for a horse pasture and set up our tents so we could leave the cabin to the packrats. Then we wrangled our horses in for the rest of our branding. Some fellas had, at some time in the past, used the place to harvest Christmas trees, hence the name "Christmas Tree Camp". And it served its purpose, saving a lot of extra miles for the horses during the month it took us to get our spring country cleaned out and branding wrapped up.

One day, I had the big idea to 'set the boys on their heels', by making a tasty beef stew. The meat we had, had proved to be some pretty tough beef. So I figured I'd put it in a pot on the coals to simmer, with some spices thrown in, and let it soften up while we were gone for the day. We had a couple tender footed dogs tied in camp, and I figured that'd keep the varmints outa the cook pot 'till we got back.

We all cut some pretty big circles that day, and had our herd bunched up, worked dries and lates out, so I left the fellas to finish mothering up the herd, while I took my horse back to camp to finish cooking my 'surprize stew'.

I rode into camp, and everything seemed normal, so I put my horse up and had a peek under the cook pot lid. Boy, that meat smelled good! I added the few spuds that we had left and whatever else that was still good and not growing hair, threw a few more spices in and let her simmer some more.

The crew rode in about an hour later, and you could just about see them drooling, it smelled so good. I knew I'd done a good job over the cook fire this time. Then it came time to dish up. We all got a plateful and dug in. Not a word was spoken, as is the way of it when cowboys only eat once in a while. It was as tasty as it smelled; all except for the meat. It was just like chewing rubber!! That's all my carefully planned cooking had done was to toughen up meat that was already tough! I chewed for a while, and I mean, it was a workout! I couldn't even get my teeth through it. I finally just got rid of it; chucked it in the general direction of the dogs, about the same time as I caught Ivan doing the same thing. Nobody said a word about the cooking, but I noticed the other fellas ridding their plates of stew meat in the same fashion. They had to. I don't think the dogs could even chew it!

I glanced at Tex, and his face was all twisted up from trying not to laugh, as he was watching someone. I followed his gaze, and there's poor old Cliff trying his level best to masticate a piece of that petrified meat, and him without a tooth in his head! It seemed like his jaws just kind of bounced apart. We watched him for a while as he was looking at the ground with his elbows braced on his

knees, really focusing on getting rid of it. That was just too much to hold in, and we all laughed like fools, and I asked Cliff if I could gather up a few rocks to throw in and help grind that thing up! He just threw it to the dogs like the rest of us had, obviously much relieved, and said "It seemed like the more I chewed it, the bigger it got!"

Chapter Twelve
Cow Camp Coffee

"It is entirely possible that a person who has seen and endured more change of life may have accumulated more wisdom."

My ol' pardner Merv and I were camped at Hungry Valley camp one summer for a while, punchin' cows around, up in the mountains at the Gang Ranch.

Mornings started with cooking breakfast by lamplight, and usually evening meals were the same. We always rode out from camp as the sun was just coming up over the horizon; that way, you got your cattle gathered and moved before the day warmed up too much. Otherwise, you'd be fighting cows out from under the shade of the timber, as that's where they'd rather be in the hot part of the day. Our days were pretty long for a couple of weeks straight, as we were trailing stock a long ways from camp, and riding quite a ways to get back. One day Merv would cook supper, and the next day, I would. The guy who doesn't cook does the chores; like wrangling horses in and catching up for the next day, packing in firewood and water, and making sure the lanterns are fueled up for the next morning.

Now everybody has got their own idea of how coffee should be done, but in camp, it's not like a restaurant; you have what's made or go without. And in camp, there'a coffee 'pot'. That's it. You put water in it, you add the ground coffee to your taste (usually a handful), get it on the verge of a boil, just rolling, take it off the fire, give it a bit of a stir, pour a half cup of cold water over it to settle the grounds, and pour it. Simple. And good. Cooked coffee.

For the next batch, Merv and I liked to just add more water; up to the 'high water mark', and a few more fresh grounds to the cooked grounds from the day before. And in a few days, it was a nice pot of coffee. And it saved on coffee grounds, so you were assured of not running out. (In cow camp, you hate to waste anything, as a fella never knows when the next load of supplies are coming up.) Usually, each week a fella would start a fresh pot.

The first day's coffee is definitely not as good as the third or fourth day's coffee. (These days I use a French press, and it reminds me a lot of the taste of that cooked coffee, but I sure waste a lot more grounds.)

Since we were putting in longer days than ever on horseback, we cooked that particular batch of coffee a little longer than usual; I reckon maybe seven or eight days. We noticed that the grounds were starting to 'break down' and we thought maybe it's just been cooked too long; although it still tasted just fine.

Well, we figured we'd just build a fresh pot the next day. But the next day was longer than the one before, and we were just glad to get our chores done at the end of the day, get some grub in our bellies and go to sleep. So the next morning, we heated up our coffee, added to it again and drank it, whether it seemed fuzzy or not, and rode out again.

Finally we got to camp with plenty of daylight left, and it was my turn to cook supper. I thought it would be a good time to clean the pot and start a fresh pot in the morning. I went outside to dump the pot away from the cabin, rinse it out and refill it at the creek. When I dumped the pot, I was a bit surprised to see a little naked mouse in the grounds! He appeared to be sorta 'rendered down'. Neither Merv nor I would have noticed he was there if I hadn't cleaned the pot to start a fresh batch...although we really didn't think he made the coffee taste at all bad!

I guess the little fella figured he needed a mineral bath; like when some people go to health spas and soak in the healing waters. Maybe he reckoned we were super human, keeping the hours we did, and thought it had something to do with the coffee!

Chapter Thirteen
Flapjacks and Syrup...Or Not

*"**Regarding Gene Huber**: After knowing Gene better, it seems almost impossible for him to tell a lie, when the truth is so readily available."*

Sherry and Gene Huber told me a story about Sherry's Dad, Russ Turnbull. Russ had told me a few stories himself, from time to time, but this one came from Sherry and Gene, this one being hard for Gene to forget!

In 1928, in his mid-teens, Russ had come out from Ontario to BC. He had set out to the Kamloops area to find whatever job he could so he could afford to buy a saddle, a horse and a rifle. He'd worked for quite a while before he was the proud owner of these items, as a teen-aged boy would be; things that would really set him free to get out and explore.

He had heard a lot about the cattle ranges in the nearby Nicola valley while working in Kamloops, and that was his goal as he set out on his ride; to find work on the ranches in the Nicola valley.

Russ was about out of grub, and was, like the old timers termed it, 'riding the grub line'. He rode through the Knutsford region, south of Kamloops, one Sunday morning. He was enjoying the scenery, and the morning sun shining down on the hills of bunchgrass, and would have been appreciating it more, I suppose, if his belly button wasn't rubbing on his backbone; the way it often is with young fellas.

The trail he was riding along was heading towards a log cabin in the hills, and as he got closer, he could smell food cooking; no doubt causing the inner man to really start kicking up a fuss. As he rode past the cabin, he was having troubling thoughts about maybe not being invited in for breakfast, when, sure enough, an older fella steps out of the doorway and greets Russ. "Good mornin' young fella! You et yet?" Russ answered he had not. "Well, go ahead and put your hoss up and come on in and have some flapjacks."

69

Russ must have figured this man was an angel, as flapjacks were his favourite. He did as the man had said: hobbled his horse up and let him graze, and he hustled into the cabin where that wonderful aroma of flapjacks cooking was coming from. No sooner had he sat down at the table, which was cluttered with everything from machine parts to bridle reins, and a real live mouse, when the old fella told him to flip his plate over, as he had a couple of big flapjacks coming his way. Russ tipped his plate sideways towards the light coming in the open doorway and sized up his plate, as his hand had encountered some crustations thereabouts. He pulled his neck rag out, or some article of clothing, and gave his plate a quick swipe, not wanting to offend the nice man who had so kindly offered a meal.

Those flapjacks sure did smell good, and they were big enough to fill a belly, Russ figured. His host pushed the tin can of Rogers Golden Syrup across the table to him, as he plopped a couple of flapjacks on Russ' plate, and said "Help yourself to the syrup!" Russ grabbed a crusty, well-used spoon, at which he 'hung an ear down' and gave it the 'hairy eyeball'; same way a spooked horse would do, because he's starting to get a wee bit unnerved with the untidy environment around that table. Russ peered into the syrup can, wondering how long the lid had been off, and there was just enough light coming in the door that there appeared to be something else in the can besides syrup!

So, he tipped it sideways to the light as well, and sure enough, there's a mouse in the syrup. Not alive. Well, that was a bit much for Russ, and he blurted out to his good host that his syrup was a might too popular; and the old timer came for a look himself. "Well, sure enough, there is too, little bugger!" And, quick as a flash, he dipped his finger in and out again, and got a hold of the mouse's tail, and with his free hand, wrapped a couple fingers around the mouse's torso and stripped his little body of the precious 'sweet stuff', back into the can! Whereupon Russ ate his flapjacks dry, exclaiming, many years later, that they were good, but forevermore wondered at that man's rash decision to strip the syrup from the mouse "against the lay of the hair", instead of with it!!

It was almost like one too many bad decisions added to a list of distasteful factors.

Chapter Fourteen
Forty and Auto

"Dogs come and go amongst the cowboy community. And every once in a while, you'll get a spell when some enterprising individual gets the idea they'd like to capitalize on some cowboy's hours of training and long days on the trail, by appropriating his dog; his working partner, pet, friend...and sometimes, maybe the dog just follows his nose off in search of excitement....??"

Our pardner Forty had himself a pup one time that disappeared like that. And there's just no way of knowing what happened to him, or where he went. Forty called this hairy little mongrel, Auto. The pup just loved riding in a truck. I don't think Forty ever had to help the pup jump in; Auto just liked riding in a truck. Auto was a half-brother, or some kind of kin to that Deefer dog ('D' fer Dog) he used to have, and darned if he didn't even look the same: hairy, with floppy ears and a big smile on his face.

One fall, when we were trailing cows down from Minnie Lake Ranch to Douglas Lake Home Ranch, Forty had this Auto pup along. I guess Auto was over a year old by this time, and past the stage where most cowdogs are showing quite a little interest in cows. He'd been trailing behind Forty's horse for a few months now. From time to time, he acted like the idea of chasing cows sorta appealed to him, but every time I saw Forty riding, Auto would be quite happily trailing along behind, with his ears flopping, long hair blowing around, and a big smile on his face.

There was one stretch of the road where we had crossed the bridge over Nicola River at Spahomin Reserve, and the road continued on past the remaining houses along Douglas Lake on our way east to the Home Ranch. There was an abandoned house, just a little square box of a house, but it was a real bright purple color, with a good round corral built about 30 feet from the front door.

Forty was riding drag past that purple house, and working hard to keep a tired drag lined out, and he was busy. Being late afternoon, the herd wanted to stop for the day. I reckon he was so busy he never noticed Auto wander off. But that was the last place he recalled seeing little Auto.

Forty drove back that evening, and for days after, looking for his dog, but no luck. He spent that fall and winter always keeping an eye open for Auto, and the rest of us fellas did too. We all kind of hoped somebody took him in and was feeding him.

Come spring, we'd all pretty much forgot about Auto, till we'd drive past that purple house again, and that would jog our memory about that smiling, hairy little fella. Anyways, winter had passed and spring came along, and the ice was breaking up on Sanctuary Lake and Douglas Lake. The geese and the new cowboys and new cooks were rolling in; we were changing up our strings and everything had a smile on its face, alive with spring.

Our cowboss, Mike Ferguson, pulled up to the cowboys' barn in his truck one Monday morning, and him and Orval had their chin-wag and when he drove away, we all swung our legs over our horses and rode out. We were making up a herd for Minnie Lake, where those cows would calve out.

Orval, the foreman at that time, shaped up the point with Jerry McKenzie; Jake Coutlee and Barry Wallace were there too. Forty and I, being the kids on the crew, naturally took up the drag, and away we went. Boy, it was a nice day; the sun was shining and a lot of the birds that were back early were in the willow trees along Douglas Lake.

When we rode past the purple house, I thought of Auto again, and turned to Forty to talk about that, and, wouldn't ya know it—there's Auto trotting behind Forty's horse! I said, in amazement, "I didn't know you found him!" "Found who!?!" blurted Forty. "Auto", I said. Forty looked at where I was pointing, stopped his horse, looked at me, looked at the dog again, in wonder, mouth agape…and sure enough, there was Auto! A little bit bigger, but none the worse for wear.

He'd just fallen in behind us on the drag, at the same place he'd left three months before. We couldn't do anything but just stare at that dog and wonder if maybe he wasn't still half in the spirit world or something. Forty piled off his horse and they had a real happy reunion, that's for sure.

73

Then, just as if to show us what he'd been thinking about all winter, Auto started herding cows back and forth and actually did look like he was trying to shape herd for a little while!

We still talk about that from time to time, and puzzle over where that dog ever disappeared to. But even more puzzling to us was the way he showed up again.

Chapter Fifteen
Mr. Bear...A Late Night Visitor

"I've found that most times, dogs, horses, men or women, will do a job better for you if you understand them well enough to know how they like (or need) to work; then let them do it that way."

When I was at Empire Valley Ranch, we'd start building our herds to go to the mountains for the summer, about mid-June. We'd build a herd of about 125 cow/calf pairs, something manageable, on those mountain trails. We would spend five days on the trail with each herd, to get them across the Camelfoot Range, and back to Relay Creek country. We'd drop them there and ride two days back home, stopping at our Yodel Camp to change up horses, pack more grub, and build another herd to trail up. The crew and I lived out of pack boxes for five or six weeks getting our herds up in those pretty mountains of Tyaughton Creek.

After we had four herds moved up to Relay Creek, two guys would stay at Relay Valley and start relaying the herds up the Tyaughton Trail. On our second night on the trail from home we camped with the herd at a spot called Chocolate Springs. Chona and Cory loose herded the girls and let them rustle around for a bellyful until dusk, while Tex, Ivan and myself rolled the beds under a big old fir tree. It was a real black looking sky, threatening to dump on us. This herd was real hard to settle for the night, and long after they were pushed in behind our brush fence for the night, they were bawling and moving around.

It got real dark that night, and we were glad to be bunked under that big tree. We stoked the fire and drank coffee late, while the herd moved around, not a hundred feet from our tree. About an hour after full dark, the herd settled down nice and we all dropped off to sleep, sort of. I think all five of us slept with one eye open that night; those girls had us a bit tight, thinking this might be a night that they bolt loose on us.

I heard that bear go 'WOOF' before I was even awake, I'm sure. When you work and sleep in the open a lot, you sleep aware, like real light. That bear must have spooked our herd worse than us, because in my sleepy state, I recall the whole herd coming to its feet at the same time and rushing our camp. I'm quite sure the only thing that kept them from boiling over top of us was every man sitting bolt upright, yelling at the top of our lungs! We must have had a good bit of help from the Head Cowboy Himself, because that herd come to a stop at our phoney brush fence!

After that, the fire was kept stoked up and the coffee pot took a workout till we broke camp. At first light, the boys started packing the horses, and I went across the creek to look for tracks of our 'midnight visitor'. Sure enough, there was griz sign along the bank of the creek. The old fella didn't want to do anything more than just amuse himself, I'm sure…Alex Rossette and Cliff Farncombe both told me that ole Mr. Bear did that once every summer, but usually the cowboys would have to ride all the way back to Grinder Meadow to catch the herd up again, two days on the trail back.

I've thought about that night quite often since, and I think my partner Tex must have been real spooked by that; being from

South Africa, he wasn't afraid of much, except for bears! I chuckle to myself still at the memory of his voice when he came awake yelling real high-pitched like a squealing pig. (I hope he doesn't write his own account of that night and what I sounded like!)

Chapter Sixteen
Dodging Logging Trucks

*"**The Temper of Steel**: I often compare a person's life, on this side of the veil, to a tempering; like that of steel. Each body that a spirit comes into must go through it's schooling; good times, hard times. Some bodies go through many hard times, maybe as many as good, and yet, the thought has come to me and stayed with me: 'the last day of our schooling is the first day of the rest of our learning'. Each hard time may be just one more class that was required for us to know. Each class we endure is another stage of the tempering process. The tempering is another way of helping us to remember.*
***Apprentice**: a person learning a craft under a skilled worker...The cowboy life can be tough at times. The apprenticeship program may seem painful from time to time for the cowboy or buckaroo, but once they are near 'full temper' the falls don't hurt near as much and the anxieties during the falls are not as frequent as they once were...This also applies to the 'falls in life'. It's a lot easier for the sun to shine, once 'tempered through'."*

Livestock and logging trucks have for years, been in each other's way on logging roads. Not that the loggers, or the cowboys, are in the wrong when it comes to using those roads. We are all tenure holders on these ranges and have our own reasons to be out there, but we need to be aware of the rules of the road.

The timber companies build these roads, and maintain them, for the most part, and place mile marker boards for radio calls to one another. It's important to look for the mile boards and know what call to make over the two way radios to alert other traffic of your whereabouts. If you don't know the roads or how to call your miles, life will get interesting for anyone making a living on those roads.

The Gang Ranch is one of those outfits that is so big, that the logging roads across parts of it, do help the cowboys access this country. Especially late in the fall, when trying to get stragglers out of the high country. And also for hauling supplies back to camps that were still in use. So, in some ways, these roads sure made a cowboy's life simpler, but sometimes not.

My pardner, Merv was hauling supplies back to Fosberry camp one fall day. Grub for the cowboys, salt for the cows, horse oats, dog food, and some hay bales. The logging road he was on was active at the time, which meant there were loaded logging trucks coming out on their way to town.

Anybody travelling on that road needed to be on their toes, so to speak. A driver definitely wants to hear the radio and be aware of those truck drivers calling their miles. On that particular road, there's a stretch the truckers called the 'narrows'. No prizes in guessing why. That stretch was about a quarter mile long, where a pickup could just possibly squeak past a logging truck—but if two logging trucks were to meet there, well, one of them would likely have to back up.

So, the radio calls were either: "14 board empty" (this logging truck would be coming in for a load of logs, or a pickup headed that same direction), or "14 board loaded" (this truck would be heading back to town). No matter if it was an empty pickup or a loaded logging truck, going in the direction of town was considered "loaded", and going in the direction away from town was considered "empty".

Now Merv had dropped off the Fosberry Camp supplies and was headed back down the road to Home Ranch Valley. The direction he was going was towards town…but he was calling his miles out as "empty".

A logging truck was coming towards him, about five or six miles away that was actually empty, and the driver was calling it that way. When they were about four miles apart and closing the distance, the truck driver contacted Merv to ask him if he might be travelling loaded…Merv replied he was empty.

Another mile swept past, and that same truck driver got on the radio, this time in earnest, to tell Merv, "uh, mister, it sounds like you're travelling loaded because I think you're getting closer to me." Again, Merv replied "But I'm empty!!"

Now Merv is a long time Gang Ranch cowboy, a top hand, and liked to consider himself, above all, a man who 'rode for the brand'. He took his job seriously. And he wasn't about to be playing games on the two way radio over something as inconsequential as what he was carrying in his truck!

Finally, the inevitable happened. They met in the narrows. Miraculously, they had a place to pass, and as Merv shoe-horned his truck past...slowly...the exasperated trucker once again mentioned to Merv that he was travelling loaded.

That was enough for Merv and he let that driver know, in no uncertain terms, that it was none of his business WHAT he was hauling in his truck! Can you imagine the shop talk that night amongst the truck drivers?!

Later that same fall, I was hauling Ryan Fritz, Cory Newton and our three horses back up that logging road to the ranching community of Big Creek. We'd gotten a report from a local rancher up there that some of our cattle had drifted in, and we were on our way to gather them up.

I had my little cowdog Polly with us, and she was riding on the floorboards because we had the one ton truck with the horse box on the back, and I sure didn't want my little buddy underfoot of those three horses. Ryan was the youngest, so he got the middle of the seat, and Cory was the 'door man'. They didn't mind sharing foot space with a dog that was to be a good fourth hand on the crew this day.

That fall, business had sure picked up with the timber companies, and there were a lot of extra trucks hauling down those roads. The extra trucks were from other parts of the province; out of town trucks. I was told there were a hundred trucks hauling three loads a day out for awhile. Maybe I was misinformed, but I really don't think so. There were a lot of trucks going up and down that road. We could only hope they all knew the mile boards.

It had been a short year since I'd had a very bad vehicle accident. And even though I mustered up the guts to get behind the wheel again, mainly through Faith, I found myself a bit uncomfortable with loaded logging trucks coming at me at the pace of one per minute.

So, white knuckled, down the road we went. Ryan, as I recall, was cracking funnies that kept the mood lightened up a bit.

But I was thinking about 'high ball dip', as the loggers referred to it, which was coming up. Us cowboys knew the area as Cow Lake, but this particular stretch of road was a wild ski jump that suddenly dipped straight down into a draw. This draw was steep enough that the drop may have two hundred yards from the brow of each side to the bottom, yet only two hundred yards from one side to the other. I knew those drivers had to have their speed up, so as to get back up the other side with a full load, without powering out and spinning out.

We'd had about 16 inches of snow on the ground, and even though the road grader kept the surface well maintained, all that traffic had turned it from compact snow into awful slippery…all in all, a great recipe for high adventure!

I was calling each and every mile in, and as we got close to 'high ball dip', we were, by this time, all keeping track of how many trucks were still close to coming from the opposite direction, as they called their miles. I had pulled over to let the last truck pass us that we had heard calling his miles within a short distance of high ball dip. From the radio calls, and there was a lot of chatter, the next truck coming at us was about four miles away.

I spoke those thoughts aloud to my pardners, and they agreed with me; there was no better time. So over the brow of the hill and down we went, keeping our speed up so as to make the other side, like we were on a toboggan run. And we made it. We were cresting the hill on the other side, with plenty of momentum to carry us over, when a loaded logging truck met us right there!

Swerving to the right, I got the passenger wheel part way in the ditch, and we barely avoided a collision by scant inches! The follies of not calling your miles! But there was no time to criticize or to be thankful for being alive. I had to back the truck up enough to get that front wheel back on the road, then try to get enough momentum to go forward and over the brow of the hill.

Putting the truck in low gear, I tried to inch forward, and we spun out. The horses shifted in the back, and we started sliding backward! The rest happened so fast; faster than it takes to tell it.

The brakes would not hold the truck at that spot. Once we started sliding backwards, she picked up speed at a really scary rate; and with the brakes on, we started to go sideways.

To tip over in that spot, with a load of horses on, and slide to the bottom, would have been fatal for someone.

I slammed the clutch down and the truck straightened out as it accelerated, free-wheeling the rest of the way to the bottom. Backwards! I was not taking much time to think; just do. Looking in the driver's side rearview mirror, I made myself focus on the truck ruts behind us, and kept it running straight backwards. We were going way too fast! But we were still upright!

Just when I felt a surge of hope that we were going to make it, the front tires grabbed a rut and that threw our front end to the left. We tipped over. Right at the bottom. But not before the momentum we had going caused the truck to slide on its left side, off the road into the passenger side ditch.

I remember hearing the horses sharp shod hooves scrambling to right themselves up on their 'new floor'. Tied to the side of the box as they were, for travelling, it would have been pretty tough for them to regain their feet.

Immediately after tipping over, another logging truck went past our front end. He was close! We could only see a flash, and he was past and gone up the other side. Our truck stopped rocking back and forth from the horses scrambling around, and by the lack of noise back there, they were either standing real still or had broken the lead shanks and were out of the truck. We would eventually find out it was the latter. I was thinking of them and expecting the worst when I felt someone step on my head. The driver's window was busted out and my left ear was driven down in the snow, as that was the side we landed on.

Then I heard Polly shrieking and my attention turned from the horses to my pardners and my dog. Ryan was hollering at Cory, "Cory! Stop! Cory, wait!" "Cory!!" He yelled, "Just wait, Polly's tail is tangled up in your spur!" I turned my head so I could see what was happening, because whoever had placed their vibram sole on my head had now removed it; and sure enough, there was little Polly, free swinging upside down and yelping, with her tail caught up in Cory's spur rowel.

Cory was already propelling himself up through the passenger side window, preparing to kangaroo out of there on coiled springs. Polly was having quite a ride!

I watched as Ryan found some footing on the dashboard, and my shoulder, to cradle Polly and unhook her from Cory's spur. When he told Cory "okay", I saw that cowboy disappear like a fly. Ryan called Cory again, and told him to take Polly. Then Ryan and I pried our way out, doing our level best to imitate Cory's kangaroo impression.

Once we were out of the truck, we saw Cory had two of the horses caught up, and I went to mine and got my hands on him. Miraculously, nobody was hurt. Horses, Polly, or us. A bit shocked for sure, but not hurt. So we did the next best thing any cowboy would do; we went into the timber a ways and got a little bonfire going to help cheer ourselves up a bit.

The truck drivers must have called in our accident, because before long, one of the foremen for the timber company stopped to see if we needed help. He got word to Gang Ranch Headquarters, and Larry, Dave and Brian came to bail us out. We were sure glad to see them. They got the truck back on his legs again, Dave checked it over and drove us home…even the truck survived without too many dings

All in all, it was another one of those cheap lessons in life. Friends were there, again, to help us; and in later years, we all had a laugh, recalling Polly's wild ride.

Chapter Seventeen
Diamond and Our December Swim

"Freedom has been my friend through this dimension, beckoning me from on top of a ridge, so that I may see what's on the other side. All my life She has appeared in many ways to me, but always in a beautiful and racy form, offering me her hand; "Come, look..." and has led me to many adventures, when environments might otherwise have become abusive or stagnant to me. Freedom has shown me excitement, awe, and occasionally stark fear; while Faith has assured me, one way or another; that I will always be looked after. And that is what gave me the confidence to trust again."

When I ran Voght Valley Ranch (a satellite ranch belonging to Nicola Ranch), I'd work for them from the first of March until the cows and yearlings were all down at headquarters in the Nicola Valley. Usually that would be the end of November, but some years the weather would lock us in for a week or so longer.

One year we had walked all the cows and yearlings out by the end of November, but I still had 30 bulls to ship out. We'd had a snow storm come in and got 24 inches of snow dumped on us inside of 48 hours. Those bulls rustled around the willows along Voght creek, and they were getting a belly full. The day after the storm let up, the roads were plowed out, and I got a call from management that a cattle liner was on its way up that afternoon.

So I saddled up Diamond. He was a nice big brown gelding, a ranch horse, about ten years old. I'd stripped the shoes off him, and planned on hauling him and a couple of other ranch horses down to headquarters after the bulls were hauled out. I took Boomer, my Catahoula dog, and we rode on down to the meadows, about a mile from the ranch buildings to start the bulls moving for the corrals. I noticed one black bull kept giving Boomer some grief; walking back to the willows to rustle for grass, as all the other bulls were headed for the corrals.

I headed Diamond over to give Boomer a hand, and hadn't gone more than about fifty feet through the snow when I stopped him. With my senses on high alert, I tried to remember where that excavator operator had dug that deep sump to drain the meadows of water late in the summer. I was sure it was close to where my horse was standing, but under two feet of snow. The snow was reflecting sunlight, and it was tough to see the mounds of dirt, especially since they'd been levelled out for the most part.

All of the sudden, I got a bad feeling in my belly. I knew it had not been cold enough to freeze that deep pond hard, and even though the temperature was minus 25 degrees on this day, there was a lot of fresh snow as insulation on top. I turned Diamond around to head for 'other parts', anywhere but there! And just that quick, we went straight through!! I tell you, my horse and I went completely under water!

I came up sputtering and trying to swim, and I came up against two feet of snow on a thin crust of ice. Just as I got something solid under my forearms, and I thought I could pull myself out, Diamond came up swimming for good ground, and his front feet caught the back of my belt and pulled me under again. I came up sputtering, and waved one arm in front of his face so he'd shy away from me and give me a chance to find something solid to pull myself out on. It sure was a bad spot I was in, because as soon as I'd try to roll myself out into that deep snow, the ice would break through again, then I'd come up, only to have Diamond follow me and pull me under again with his front feet.

Finally I got something solid under my arms again, and I think it was one of those big old swamp-grass crowns, and I was able to roll out into the snow. I rolled around in that fresh snow to help take some of the water out of my wool pants and jacket, and when I got up, I could see good ole Diamond resting at the spot where I got out, with only his head and neck showing above the water.

My poor horse; I was pretty sure there was no way to get him out, especially when I'm not sure how I got out myself. But the bridle reins were showing above the water, so I reached for them, got them, and tried giving him a pull, just to keep him trying. And he did try again, and managed to get one front foot up on solid ground. Then he tried a bit more and got the other front foot up; and now the saddle horn was visible. And that's when he just stopped trying. I talked to him and I asked God to help us, and I pulled on them little reins, knowing that wouldn't do much good. Most times when horses go into shock in water like that, they float onto their side, then there's not a lot more you can do, not without a machine or a good rope horse, that is.

Diamond must have gotten his second wind, because he started trying again, and with one big, mighty heave ho, he pulled himself out! Now a horse will never pull near as much with his shoulders the way he can with his hind quarters, just the way the shoulders are attached. And all I could do was to hang onto them flimsy bridle reins and kind of balance him forward, I guess. But, boy! Out he came, and really, none the worse for wear.

By this time, Boomer had that last bull in the track of all of his pardners, and I led Diamond down the track behind them. I got the bulls locked in the corrals, unsaddled Diamond, and covered him over with a blanket, in the barn. By the time I left him to go change out of my wet clothes, he was eating hay, and real content.

Surprisingly, he never went into shock at all; in fact, we were both right as rain.

I think about that episode a lot. And as tough as it was for me to get out of that straight sided water hole, it was downright impossible to get that horse out. I reckon the Head Cowboy Himself had something to do with that.

Glossary

BEAR SIGN: bear tracks, or scat. In some areas, also referred to as 'doughnuts'.

BRUSHED UP: wild cattle or bulls running into the brush to hide on riders, usually dogs are needed to bring them out. In hot weather, even riders will 'brush up' for a rest, for themselves and their horses.

BUCKAROO: adulterated from the Spanish word 'vaquero'; whereas pronunciation of the 'V' sounds like 'B'. The heart of buckaroo country being mostly Nevada and Oregon. 'Vaqueros' being the hands that trailed livestock up the West Coast Ranges into the Interior of BC.

CATAHOULA: a breed of dog originating on the Louisiana/Texas border. Used for trailing and catching wild cattle in rough country.

CAVVY: horse herd, or remuda.

CHANGE STRINGS: to run in the entire remuda and catch fresh mounts for all the hands. Changing strings occurs every 6-8 weeks, and those horses going back into the remuda will get 2-3 months off. Each rider will shoe up 3-4 fresh mounts which will be used for the next 6-8 weeks, until time to change strings again.

CHANGE UP: when Spring works are nearing completion, or any of the other seasons, each cowboy's mounts will need a rest of a couple months. Shoes will be stripped off. He'll get three or four fresh horses in and shoe them up for the next six or eight weeks work.

CHOUSING: another word for chasing

COOK CAR: a portable cook trailer

COUNT (the COUNT): most every herd, upon being worked or trailed, will be tallied (counted) and it is vital to keep track of the count.

COWBOSS: the boss of the cowboy crew. He is generally in charge of the cow herd and the cavvy. He will usually have a foreman under him to run the crew. The foreman is often referred to as the 'Jigger Boss' or 'Straw Boss'.

DRAG: the back end of the herd. Drag riders are responsible for making sure none of the livestock stops to graze, and none of the calves turn back to run away, thereby being left behind. You can't push a chain from the back; momentum begins at the front. Usually

89

the least experienced hands ride the drag, and the most seasoned hands go to the forward positions. The riders on drag will gain experience moving cattle and learn to work as a crew.

DRIES: refers to a cow without a calf. In direct reference to the cow's udder. A cow with a calf being 'wet'.

FALL WORKS: in reference to cow herds, when gathering cattle from summer range and trailing them home. As well, weaning calves from their mothers, and shipping them. Or in the case of yearling outfits, the calves then go through the chute for vaccinations, etc. and into the feedlot for the winter.

FLANK: when trailing herds, the position behind the swing riders. Flank riders are mostly responsible for keeping the drag from getting too wide across. They position themselves in front of the widest part of the herd, so those cows move in more towards the center line following the trail. This only works well if the drag riders stop momentarily to allow the cows to come back onto the trail. This encourages a herd that is 'lined out' , which keeps cattle cooler, and makes the herd more efficient to move.

FORKED: pertaining to the rider who is hard to buck off.

HOBBLED: hobbles are made of either rope or leather, and will be tied around the front legs of the horse, below the knee. Its beneficial to teach a horse to stand hobbled and wait for their rider.

JINGLE BOB: small bits of forged metal, similar in appearance to the clapper in a bell, used for a similar result; to chime against the rowel of the spur. "Cowboy Music"…some cowboys like them, some don't.

LATES: cows calving later than others, bred on a later cycle. It is more productive, and economically feasible to have cattle calving in the same window of time, as opposed to having them calve spread out over the months.

LINED OUT: regarding a cow herd, walking down the trail, mostly in a long strung out herd, as opposed to a tightly bunched mob. Also, in regard to cowboys; on a long trot or lope, and going someplace.

MOTHERING UP: herd work; before and after trailing a herd of cows to a new part of the range, the herd will be gathered to a level ground where the crew will circle the herd and hold them in that spot. The cowboss, or foreman will ride into the herd and sort, or part out cows that have been able to find their babies in the melee.

Herds are generally from about 150-300 pairs (cow/calf pairs), and it's difficult for calves to be able to stay close to their mother at all times. If a herd is not mothered up, the calves who can't immediately find their mothers will run all the way back to the last place they nursed. The cow will also follow back later, in search of their calf.

OPEN STRING: all the horses in the 'cavvy' or 'remuda' not being in a cowboy's particular string. Perhaps a cowboy has left the outfit; thus the shoes will be stripped off the horses and the horses 'turned out'; they are now considered in the 'open string'.

PAIRING OFF: same as mothering off; parting off pairs. Separating pairs from the rest of the herd.

PARTING OFF: referring to parting dry cows from a herd of pairs (wet cows). Or sorting off strays (neighbor's cattle), parting off steers from heifers. Sorting.

POINT: when trailing cattle, there are titles to determine positions, in relationship to the herd, where cowboys will ride. The cowboy, or buckaroo, will be responsible for riding this position for the duration of the ride, to avoid having riders galloping about madly through and around the herd, and suddenly changing positions, thereby sending the cattle into a state of panic. The 'point' is the position of being in the front, the lead, and is always ridden by the cowboss or an experienced hand. It is akin to the head of the arrow.

PREG-CHECK: each cow in the herd will be pregnancy checked during fall works to determine whether she will have a calf, and whether or not it will be late. The added expense of wintering a cow not in calf, or calving too late is bad for the bottom line.

PUNCHED COWS: (punching cows). Moving cows, on the trail, to better feed and water, to summer range, or home again in the fall. This term originated in the 1800's when cattle were shipped by railcar, and the cowboys would move from car to car poking (punching) the steers, or cows with long poles to get them back on their feet, if they were down (to keep them from being trampled), or to move them ahead.

PUNCHY: in some instances, referring to a person overly fatigued; in regards to cowboys, it depicts more the gear and apparel; having attractive, quality gear and apparel; looking very much 'The Hand".

RELAY HERDS: when moving big herds over long distances, one method of trailing them over a period of several days is to have one crew trail them the first day to a spot with good feed. Then, the next day, a second crew will gather them and trail them further along.

RODEAR GROUNDS: a place, or area, designated by the cowboss or jigger boss, where all riders will gather cattle to. At this spot, sometimes referred to as the 'mothering ground'; cow/calf pairs will be paired off, or dries parted off.

ROLLERS: in reference to the bit; the 'roller' is built into the mouthpiece, shaped to make a sound like a cricket, when the horse rolls it with his tongue. This tends to pacify most horses, making the bit more acceptable to the horse, and also serves to keep the mouth wet, especially when made with copper.

ROPING OUT HORSES: when catching up horses; if running in 30 horses or more, it is advantageous to teach them to stand up facing a rope, or corral, and throw a loop over their heads to catch them. Horses running at random around a corral jockey for position, and the boss horses sometimes rough up the others, which can result in back bites and other injuries. Thus it is helpful to train them to be 'roped out'.

SABE: Spanish for 'savvy'; to understand or to know

SHIP OUT: to load cattle on stock liners to be delivered to far parts of the ranch, or sale stock being loaded for market.

SORTING: done on the range, or in corrals, by mounted cowboys. Separating certain animals from the herd, ie, 'sorting' out the neighbour's stock, or dries from a herd of cow/calf pairs, or heifers from steers.

STRAGGLE: part of fall works with the cow herd. The last of the cattle left on the range after most of the herd has been gathered in. When found, these 'stragglers' are 'straggled in'.

STRINGS (OF HORSES): each cowboy, when hired on the outfit, will be designated a number of horses for him only. This is referred to as his 'string'. Newer hands generally begin with 5-6 in their string, while older hands accumulate as many as 8-9.

STRIP SHOES: to pull off shoes and trim the horse's feet, in preparation for turning out the horse.

SWING: the position a rider takes, when moving herd, which is behind the point rider. The point riders bend the point of the herd in a new direction; swing riders assist from behind to ensure the rest of the herd follows.

WEAN CALVES: to sort calves from their mothers, usually on a permanent basis. This is part of fall works, often referred to as 'weaning time'.

WHISTLE STRING: better known as a 'stampede string'. In the case of the 'Whistle String', it was a source of amusement, referring to a child's cowboy hat, complete with a whistle on the end of the stampede string. The stampede string keeps the cowboy's hat in place when it's windy, or when racing through the country on horseback.

WRANGLE: to run the cavvy in on horseback, so cowboys can change mounts, or catch their mounts for the day. Also known as 'to jingle the horses in'.

YEARLING RANGE: for outfits that keep calves to sell on the yearling market, yearling steers or heifers will be brought to a summer range, separate from cow/calf range. They are gathered later and trailed down to market, usually the first part of September, before fall works (gathering the main herd in to wean and put on feed) begins.

In the world of cowboys, there is generally not a lot of time for long explanations, when on the job. This is where a word may have two or more meanings; but would say as much as a sentence. This particular word may be accompanied by a grunt. Or the cowboy may only receive a grunt. Possibly, depending on the circumstance, a cowboy may only receive a scornful glare.

The scornful glare can be a very moving experience. Sometimes putting a cowboy into a week-long state of depression...Most cowboys would sooner take a beating than the scornful glare, because without actual verbal abuse, it's anyone's guess as to the level of scorn the senior hand may have for said cowboy.

Cows too, can give that same look. As can horses when they've run hard after a cow critter that is in need of a rope necklace and then the cowboy misses that shot!

93

Ah! The language we speak, English, or what have you; where would it be without careful consideration to body language.

Epilogue

We thought we had moved on from the outfits. But deep inside I realized we were feeling like two old horses that the wranglers had run in with the rest of the cavvy. They shipped the other horses out, and we were free to 'take the gate', and wander where we would.

It took a few years of me looking, and my buddy waiting, for me to pick my trail. And finally, I can say I'm looking for a new Range.

In early morning light, or close of the day, I sit at my desk and I look past my lamp through the window at the snowflakes falling. Beyond them, through them, I see our horses…waiting. They've already been fed, so what are they waiting for? Waiting for spring? Waiting for the time to come when they can help this human again? Perhaps waiting for him to find his trail.

As I watch them, I think of the many miles and adventures they have taken me to. All the faces of cowboys and cowgirls I have ridden with, some still in this dimension, many gone on to the next. I see those faces on the walls in my little space in this loft.

And I think of the horse. There will always be the horse. He has carried the human through many great adventures. We have built civilizations with the horse, and then torn them down. The horse will always help with whatever we need.

The horse could be just another four legged creature, standing out on the prairie with the wind blowing his mane and tail, or he could be in a little makeshift corral getting acquainted with someone. One thing may lead to another, and pretty soon there's a boy or a girl up on his back. It's possible the horse may spook, and maybe the youngster falls to the ground. It is what it is, a learning experience, and the human doesn't learn anything by not doing something.

Now the human is a bit wiser. This bit of wisdom helps us to understand the horse better. Some of the most successful people I have known have dusted themselves off again somewhere along their trail.

The human, however, really stumbles if he can't forgive himself. God forgives…and we can too. We start again, and we are easier on everything around us, including the horse. And this puts us in a better place to be able to pass knowledge along to others. To some boy or girl that's looking up at us with wide eyes. The way I was. The way many of us were.